ADHD WORKBOOK
FOR
WOMEN

FROM CHAOS TO CONTROL: A COMPREHENSIVE GUIDE TO MAXIMIZE YOUR POTENTIAL AND OVERCOME ADHD CHALLENGES AS A WOMAN

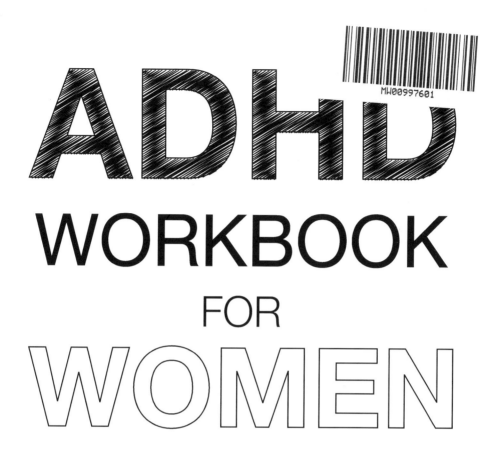

RACHEL FREEMAN

IPPOCERONTE
publishing

TABLE OF CONTENTS

INTRODUCTION

*I*n 2020, a study conducted for the Global Health Epidemiology Reference Group estimated that globally, there are more than 370 million people with ADHD. Looking at these statistics, it's no surprise that there are now countless books available on the subject.

ADHD is a global problem that has only begun to be tracked and recognized as it should in recent years. However, if we analyze the population of those with ADHD, we discover that women are the minority. According to the Centers for Disease Control and Prevention (CDC), 12.9% of men and boys live with ADHD compared to 5.6% of women and girls.

Why is that? Why are men more likely to be diagnosed with ADHD than women?

There are various reasons. For instance, hyperactivity at school-age is more easily diagnosed in males than females. Attention deficit, on the other hand, is more complex to analyze. In addition, girls tend to be generally quieter, and many schools ignore the problem or are not equipped to identify ADHD symptoms. As a result, diagnosis is delayed for years, and sometimes the problem is never identified.

The issue with this imbalance in the diagnosed population is that the treatment methods are mainly geared toward male representatives. Most of the books on the market treat ADHD as a singular problem with little variance between genders.

However, this is not representative of reality—ADHD impacts our lives in extremely different ways, and it is impossible to write a helpful book for everyone. If we take, for example, an ADHD coach, the methods and suggestions they will share with their clients could differ significantly based on multiple factors, one of which being gender:

> *"Research shows that ADHD exacts a greater toll on women than it does on men. Clinicians need a different set of tools for diagnosing and treating the disorder across genders—and women deserve a better understanding of how the disorder affects them. [...] Women with ADHD face many of the same symptoms as their male counterparts, it's true—but they also labor under the added burden of restrictive gender roles, fluctuating hormones, and a greater tendency towards self-doubt and self-harm."* (Littman, 2022)

When I was diagnosed with ADHD, I was already in high school, and my academic results were shaky. The support I received during the first few years of university helped me understand the importance of early diagnosis and how each person deals with ADHD differently.

Throughout my career, I have worked with countless clients and seen various facets of ADHD. This helped me learn how men and women experience this problem differently and require different approaches. While their symptoms may be similar, in the long term, women and men with ADHD can face significantly different outcomes.

The reason I wrote this book is to provide support to all women who have ADHD. It is for those who want to try new battle-tested methods and approaches, starting from a book written for the female population.

PLEASE REMEMBER THAT THIS VOLUME IS NOT A SUBSTITUTE FOR YOUR DOCTOR OR THE MEDICINES YOU ARE TAKING. THIS IS ONLY A GUIDE DESIGNED TO ADDRESS THE MOST COMMON PROBLEMS A WOMAN WITH ADHD MAY ENCOUNTER DAILY.

The chapters in this book are self-contained, and you can consume them in any order you like. I still suggest you read them in order, but I understand that not all the issues outlined here may resonate with you.

ADHD is so complex that the problems we face are incredibly diverse, and how we experience them varies from person to person. For this reason, I apologize in advance if some of the suggestions in this book seem obvious or not incredibly useful for your case.

My intention was to write a guide that can help as many women as possible who live with this problem, and I hope that everyone can benefit from this book in some way by using these ideas and methods to help them improve their everyday lives.

Being a self-publisher, I wanted to provide this book at an affordable price to be accessible to everyone. Therefore, having only a certain number of pages available, I have chosen to include the QR codes and links to a series of online resources at the end of some chapters that you can print if you wish. I hope you enjoy this bonus content!

The resources and planners in this workbook are also available online. Go to page 142 for more information.

Without further ado, it's time to dive into what I hope will be your go-to guide to battling ADHD!

CHAPTER 1

EXECUTIVE FUNCTIONS

I decided to start this book not with a series of exercises but with a few fundamental concepts. The main reason for this is that I want everyone to understand why I recommend specific methodologies instead of others and how our ADHD brains work.

So let me start by introducing the concept of executive functions. If you feel already confident about this subject, feel free to skip this chapter and move to the next!

Allow me to quote two famous academic articles written in 2013 and 2020, respectively, that give a perfect definition of what executive functions are:

> *"Executive functions (EFs) make possible mentally playing with ideas; taking the time to think before acting; meeting novel, unanticipated challenges; resisting temptations; and staying focused. Core EFs are inhibition [response inhibition (self-control—resisting temptations and resisting acting impulsively) and interference control (selective attention and cognitive inhibition)], working memory, and cognitive flexibility (including creatively thinking "outside the box," seeing anything from different perspectives, and quickly and flexibly adapting to changed circumstances)."* (A., 2013)

"The executive system includes a broad range of processes associated with the prefrontal and thalamic-reticular areas of the brain, responsible for directing and regulating cognitions, emotions, and behaviour in order to reach a desired goal. There is evidence that [Executive Functions] EF deficits may be core components of the complex neuropsychology of ADHD. Support for this proposal can be found in the EF impairments that have been identified in adults with ADHD." (Roselló B., 2020)

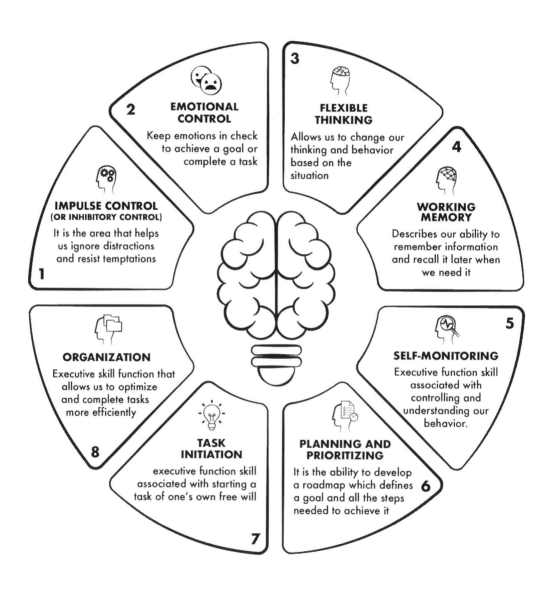

3 FLEXIBLE THINKING
Allows us to change our thinking and behavior based on the situation

2 EMOTIONAL CONTROL
Keep emotions in check to achieve a goal or complete a task

IMPULSE CONTROL (OR INHIBITORY CONTROL) 1
It is the area that helps us ignore distractions and resist temptations

4 WORKING MEMORY
Describes our ability to remember information and recall it later when we need it

5 SELF-MONITORING
Executive function skill associated with controlling and understanding our behavior.

ORGANIZATION 8
Executive skill function that allows us to optimize and complete tasks more efficiently

TASK INITIATION 7
executive function skill associated with starting a task of one's own free will

PLANNING AND PRIORITIZING 6
It is the ability to develop a roadmap which defines a goal and all the steps needed to achieve it

In conclusion, executive functions are mental processes that allow people to make plans and stay focused. Therefore, a disorder in any part of these processes could cause ADHD.

There are eight main executive functions (even if some studies have identified a larger number of them), and each deals with a specific area. Let's take a look at them here in detail:

1. **Impulse control** (or **inhibitory control**) is the area that helps us ignore distractions and resist temptations. Efficient impulse control leads us to think before we act.

2. **Emotional control** is keeping emotions in check to achieve a goal or complete a task. It allows us to remain calm under pressure, manage anxiety, and not be immediately frustrated or unhappy when things don't go as we expect. Emotional control is the ability to handle disruptive emotions and impulses to control your actions and decisions.

3. **Flexible thinking** allows us to switch from one task to another, adapt to the environment, and change our thinking and behavior based on the situation. People who have no problem with flexible thinking can switch from a pleasant to a less enjoyable activity when necessary. A person with flexible thinking can change strategies along the way. If a first approach doesn't work as hoped and seems doomed to fail, this person will switch to a different approach.

4. **Working memory** describes our ability to remember information and recall it later when we need it. Just like a computer, our brains can store only a certain amount of data in the short term. Working memory is generally associated with reading, performing mathematical operations, and following complex instructions that require multiple steps.

5. **Self-monitoring** is an executive function skill associated with controlling and understanding our behavior. For example, at work or school, this could mean identifying mistakes and reviewing them, or changing our behavior to avoid repeating them later. A person equipped with self-monitoring has less disruptive behaviors, can carry out tasks in sequence more efficiently, and tends to listen and cooperate more, proving to be a good team player.

6. **Planning and prioritizing** is an executive function that acts on a generally more distant time horizon. It is the ability to develop a roadmap which defines a goal and all the steps needed to achieve it. Thanks to this ability, we can manage long-term projects, define our goals, and avoid being constantly stuck in the details of a task, losing sight of the big picture. In addition, the ability to prioritize allows us to decide what is important at that moment instead of trying to work on multiple tasks at the same time.

7. **Task initiation** is the executive function skill associated with starting a task of one's own free will. This ability is generally associated with generating ideas independently and reacting to instructions autonomously without having to rely on the support of others. People who don't have problems with task initiation can follow daily routines without any problems. Furthermore, they know where to start a task without resorting to external support.

8. **Organization** is the executive skill function that allows us, by observing the environment, to optimize and complete tasks more efficiently. Organization skills are often closely tied to the ability to plan and prioritize. In addition, the organization skill comes into play in how we perform physical tasks, like tidying up a room, and this ability directly impacts how we express ourselves, structure our speech, and communicate.

We now know what executive functions are and why they are essential to women with ADHD. Given the focus of this book, I won't go into further detail on this topic, but there is some interesting reading I can suggest if you wish to delve further into the subject:

- Russel A. Barkley (2012). *Executive Functions: What They Are, How They Work, and Why They Evolved*

- Diamond A. (2013). Executive functions. *Annual Review of Psychology*, pages 135–168. You can find it online on the National Library of Medicine's website at https://www.ncbi.nlm.nih.gov/pmc/articles/PMC4084861. It is such a great article that I quoted its abstract at the opening of this chapter.

CHAPTER 2

ADHD AND EXERCISE

We all know that exercise is supposed to be good for us, and we are all sick of hearing about it. The thing is, most of us, strangely, don't do 30 to 60 minutes of it three to six times a week.

There are plenty of reasons for that, and I've probably used each of these excuses at least a hundred times. Too tiring, too boring, too busy, abs are for people with nothing better to do, etc. It is not that we are not trying, right? But we always have more important stuff to do, and in general, it is tough to stick to a regular exercise routine, and the executive function challenges that come with ADHD can make it exceptionally difficult.

Also, ADHD schedules can be pretty hectic, and self-care activities like exercise are often neglected when we get busy. I'm not an exception, especially at the beginning of my career; I decided that spending extra hours with books, scientific papers, and customers was more important than taking care of myself.

What we all forgot to factor in is that exercise is not only for the body; it is also incredible for the brain, including ADHD brains!

Now, you could ask yourself: Is it worth the effort to work out just for the brain benefits? The short answer is yes.

The longer answer is, according to Patrick LaCunt's and Cynthia Hartung's studies in 2018:

> *"There are numerous reasons for mental health providers to recommend it as an adjunct to psychosocial and pharmacological treatments. We reviewed several promising prospects for research into physical exercise interventions for emerging adults with ADHD."* (LaCunt & Hartung, 2018)

To keep it simple, when you exercise, you have some short-term benefits; your body releases what we informally call "happy chemicals," a.k.a. endorphins. You also receive a boost in dopamine and norepinephrine; these are the same neurotransmitters that medication increases to help us focus. This is the main reason why, after a good workout, your level of happiness and productivity will increase.

There are also long-term brain benefits; exercising increases the production of a protein called BDNF. This protein promotes a brain process called neurogenesis, which creates new brain cells (Yau, Gil-Mohapel, Christie, & So, 2014). So when you exercise, you are literally growing your brain.

Research suggests that at least 30 minutes of moderate to high intensity exercise produces the most neurotransmitters and BDNF, but every form of exercise helps our brains at different levels.

Whatever leads us to move our body is good; that's the main point. If you don't want to run outside, don't do it. If you hate spending time on a treadmill, don't even try.

Instead, do what you like and start from your interests.

Do you like dogs? Go for a walk with your best friend or volunteer in a dog shelter.

Do you like to learn new stuff? What about a tennis or golf lesson? Have you ever tried climbing? The possibilities are limitless!

Once you have figured out what you like and are ready to commit, you should consider a few other factors. The biggest one is your ADHD brain, which will obviously get in the way.

For a woman without ADHD, regularly exercising is about fighting her laziness; in our case, our brains will create many barriers, and laziness is just one of them.

We don't even think about all the things that may get in our way. There are those barriers that exist for every person, like: "Today was terrible, I'm tired," or "I don't have time, I have other stuff to do." But there are more specific obstacles for us, and we tend to face them while others don't.

For instance, we could face sensory barriers. Some of us, myself included, are hypersensitive to touch (tactile defensiveness). Small things like weights hurting our hands or clothes fitting too tight can lead to high discomfort and anxiety. If you are like me, you suffer from Restless Legs Syndrome (RLS), and you may develop an unconscious rejection of wearing tight gym clothes without even realizing that this is the barrier you are facing.

There are also time management barriers. Women with ADHD often work long hours to accomplish the same things that people without ADHD do. For some of my clients, it started in high school with spending extra time doing their homework and realizing they didn't have enough time to go out and play. Others had to drop activities they liked because the time was never enough. All these ADHD barriers work together to make it difficult for us to work out.

Some people spend a lot of money on expensive classes and personal trainers to get a certain level of support. This may work in the short term, but it is hardly economically sustainable in the long term.

For myself, in the past, this led to depression cycles. I was paying for expensive PT to do my exercises, but I would regularly run out of money after a few months. At that point, I would lose that extra support and direction and drop my gym schedule after a few solo sessions. This was repeating in cycles, giving me a horrible sense of wasting my time while constantly having to start over.

Last but not least, there is another barrier, which is having to deal with emotional dysregulation, impatience, and getting frustrated easily. This doesn't include all people with ADHD, but many of my clients and I have trouble with delayed gratification. We work with shorter time horizons: "I've been training for two weeks, and I don't see any results!"

What I've learned to do is try to get rid of as many barriers as I can. It won't be perfect, but it makes life easier. Removing enough barriers makes exercising a doable activity, even for us. Here are some key areas that will help you maintain regular training.

EQUIPMENT AND CLOTHING

We should start by accepting that some of the equipment and clothing people without ADHD use won't work well for us. This doesn't mean we have to buy a personalized gym, but some minor changes can help us struggle less with a training session.

For instance, for a while, I was using one of those thin yoga mats like everyone else in my class. Eventually, I got a thick, soft one because it feels better to me from a sensory perspective. My gym clothing doesn't follow fashion; it has to be comfortable. Tight clothes drive me crazy, so I buy large, soft cotton clothes, and I have one less thing to think about.

A client of mine struggles with using metallic weights; they don't feel right in her hands. So, she bought some colorful rubber weights for training that don't trigger a sensory reaction.

Also, if you train at home, try to store all your equipment in a single place to avoid jumping from one place to another to get all your gear.

ACCOUNTABILITY

Another thing I found personally helpful is accountability. I've wasted mornings trying to convince myself to go out for a run or lying on my yoga mat, not doing much. Sometimes it is just hard to get the motivation if you are alone. If you are the only one responsible for doing an activity, it is easy to just not do it. It becomes easier to stick to a schedule if you have a tennis buddy or someone counting on you to show up.

It is normal sometimes not to be motivated enough to do something; in these moments, being accountable for something forces us to push harder and try.

PREPARATION

Don't wait till the last minute to get started. If you have to go to the gym but your bag is not ready and your towel is nowhere to be found, you will likely stay home staring at the ceiling. Instead, while feeling motivated, pack your bag and prepare your gym program ahead of time. Make things easy on yourself, so the only thing left to do when it is time is grab your bag and go! If it is easier to go than cancel, you are more likely to go!

Also, it will help if you make anything that is part of your preparation part of your routine also.

Let me tell you a story about a young me. One day, I felt strangely motivated and decided to go for a jog.

Before going out, I decided to wash my face. I squeezed the face lotion on my hand and then realized I had to put my hair back.

So I went to get my hair clip and realized I could not put it on one-handed; I washed the face lotion off my hand and put it on.

I realized I was thirsty and went to the kitchen to get some juice. I noticed that the orange juice was almost gone as I poured it, so I decided to stop by the supermarket after the jog and buy some more. I went to the bedroom to get my wallet.

Passing the corridor, I looked in the mirror and noticed that my pink top didn't look great on me. I then opened the wardrobe to look for an alternative. Unfortunately, I immediately remembered that most of my gym clothes were dirty. While I was thinking about what to wear, I decided that I could still do a load of laundry while I was out.

I got the laundry basket and started loading the washing machine with light-colored clothes.

Among the dirty things, I found my armband that I use while running to hold my cell phone.

I decided it didn't look dirty and could use it one more time before washing it. My earphones were in my car; I could quickly grab them.

As I was leaving to get them, I saw the glass of orange juice on the kitchen table and realized that:

- I was thirsty.
- I didn't wash my face.
- I was still wearing the pink top.
- My wallet was still somewhere in the bedroom.
- I didn't finish loading the washing machine.
- I didn't want to go for a jog anymore.

When I say that the preparation phase for physical activity should be part of your routine, I am not joking. If I had had a simple step-by-step checklist that day, I probably would have been able to go for a run instead of constantly jumping from one thing to another.

NOVELTY

It is easy for us to get bored. Even if it is something we like, mixing it up and adding some new stuff is essential. For example, you could buy a new outfit, try different exercises, or change your workout location. Whatever is needed, don't get bored and commit to a healthy routine.

I always keep a couple of spare activities in my back pocket. I like running, but sometimes it's too cold or I don't want to do it. Luckily, I have a group of friends who are always hanging out at a bouldering gym, so when I don't feel like running, I go find them. Bouldering is not my thing, but it is hard not to get pressured into climbing some walls when I hang out with them.

EXERCISE AT A REGULAR TIME

I know it is hard. Life keeps throwing curve balls at us. There are commitments, people to see, and things to do. There is never enough time, but we have to make an effort to commit to a regular time for physical activity; otherwise, we will just forget about it and do other stuff that we think is more important.

Since I'm a morning person, I have a slot in my schedule blocked in the early morning, but you can pick whatever time of the day works best for you; just stick to it.

Don't worry; I know that for a woman with ADHD, following a schedule is brutal. For this reason, I have dedicated an entire chapter to time management and creating your routine.

We will see this topic in more detail later!

REWARD YOURSELF

It doesn't need to be something big, but it does help associate positive feelings with training.

In my case, after a good run, I always stop at my favorite coffee place. Your reward can be anything, like having a nice, long, relaxing bath instead of the usual quick shower, watching a movie after the workout, or even buying yourself a nice treat on your way home.

TRACK YOUR ACTIVITY

The most important things to track during your gym activity are not how many reps you did in your last session or your current weight. This information is generally useful but doesn't help with ADHD-specific challenges. Of course, you can keep track of it, but we should mainly focus on the four points below:

- what you did

- for how long

- how enjoyable it was

- how it affected the aspects you want to improve and focus on

To give you an example, I mainly track my sleep and productivity; for this reason, I keep a diary where, among other stuff, I usually write something like:

10/03/2022 - 4 MILES RUNNING IN AROUND 32 MINUTES - NICE PACE; I DIDN'T PUSH TOO MUCH. I HAD A COUPLE OF GOOD PRODUCTIVE HOURS IN THE MORNING AND WROTE SOME PARAGRAPHS OF THE NEW BOOK. FALLING ASLEEP WAS EASY; I DIDN'T WAKE UP UNTIL MORNING.

EXERCISE TIME!

First, I want you to write down the **barriers** you've faced in the past when you tried to exercise.

There is no immediate solution for every barrier we face. Sometimes, we must keep going even if the situation is not optimal. For other obstacles, however, we can plan our responses and try to remove them before they hinder us.

I want you to write out your plan to eliminate the barriers you listed above (when possible).

Considering how to remove a barrier between us and our goals is a fundamental part of the exercise. Don't be surprised if this takes time; realizing a barrier exists and thinking about how to deal with it is not easy.

BARRIER	POTENTIAL SOLUTION

BARRIER	POTENTIAL SOLUTION

BARRIER	POTENTIAL SOLUTION

If you can't find a solution to some of the barriers listed above, I've included a table containing my clients' most common challenges and how we decided to address them.

Unfortunately, I cannot provide the personalized support that each of you deserves through this book, but I hope that some of the problems you are facing are addressed here.

BARRIER	POTENTIAL SOLUTION
GYM CLOTHES ARE UNCOMFORTABLE	THERE IS NO NEED TO BE TRENDY. LOOSE-FITTING COTTON CLOTHING IS PERFECT FOR TRAINING. GIVE IT A TRY!
LIFTING WEIGHTS AND FITNESS IS NOT MY THING, AND I'M NOT MOTIVATED TO COMMIT TO IT. MOREOVER, I GET QUICKLY BORED WITH REPETITIVE STUFF.	HAVE YOU CONSIDERED A GROUP ACTIVITY LIKE BASKETBALL OR SOCCER? IF YOU ARE UNCOMFORTABLE WITH LARGE GROUPS OF PEOPLE, YOU COULD TRY A 1:1 SPORT LIKE TENNIS.
I'M ALWAYS LATE WHEN IT IS TIME TO GO TO THE GYM. SO, IN MOST CASES, I DON'T BOTHER TO GO BECAUSE I WON'T HAVE ENOUGH TIME TO DO MY WORKOUT.	YOUR WORKOUT CAN BE FLEXIBLE. IF YOU DON'T HAVE ENOUGH TIME TO DO IT ALL, YOU CAN TRY TO DO ONLY A PART OF IT OR GO FOR A QUICK JOG. IT WILL STILL HELP YOU DEVELOP YOUR ROUTINE. FURTHERMORE, TO BETTER MANAGE YOUR TIME AND FOLLOW A SCHEDULE, I SUGGEST YOU READ THE CHAPTER DEDICATED TO TIME MANAGEMENT.
I IMPULSIVELY COMMITTED TO SOMETHING ELSE, AND NOW I'M UNABLE TO FOLLOW MY TRAINING SCHEDULE.	BEING IMPULSIVE IS A COMMON FEATURE IN WOMEN WHO HAVE ADHD. I ADVISE YOU TO READ THE HOW TO SAY "NO" CHAPTER. YOU MAY FIND SOME USEFUL TECHNIQUES TO DEAL WITH THIS PROBLEM.

BARRIER	POTENTIAL SOLUTION
SENSORY OVERLOAD AT THE GYM KILLS ME. ALSO, THE CLANKING OF THE METAL EQUIPMENT IS IRRITATING.	IF YOUR PROBLEM ONLY CONCERNS THE AUDITORY SPHERE, YOU COULD TRY USING NOISE-CANCELING HEADPHONES. IF THE PROBLEM IS MORE EXTENSIVE, YOU COULD TRY SPORTS THAT DON'T TAKE PLACE IN GYMS. SWIMMING IS VERY RELAXING FOR SOME PEOPLE, OR EVEN A SIMPLE RUN OUTDOORS
I THINK I'M NOT GOOD ENOUGH, I'M NOT DOING THE EXERCISES CORRECTLY, AND EVERYONE IS LOOKING AT ME.	IF YOU DON'T FEEL COMFORTABLE PERFORMING BODYWEIGHT EXERCISES, SEVERAL GYM MACHINES ALLOW YOU TO DO GUIDED EXERCISES. IF YOU DON'T KNOW HOW TO DO AN EXERCISE, YOU COULD HIRE A PERSONAL TRAINER FOR A FEW LESSONS TO LEARN THE PROPER TECHNIQUE. IF THE PROBLEM IS TOO MANY PEOPLE IN THE GYM, TRY GOING OFF-PEAK IF YOU CAN. IF ALL THIS DOESN'T WORK, SIMPLE PHYSICAL ACTIVITIES LIKE RUNNING, CYCLING, OR EVEN WALKING YOUR DOG CAN HELP.
I'M NOT GOOD AT FOLLOWING INSTRUCTIONS OR REMEMBERING ANY SPORT'S RULES UNDER PRESSURE. I'M AFRAID I WILL MAKE A FOOL OF MYSELF.	THERE ARE A LOT OF SPORTS WITH VERY FEW RULES. ICE SKATING, FOR EXAMPLE, CAN BE LEARNED IN 1:1 SESSIONS, AND ONCE YOU KNOW THE BASICS, NOBODY FORCES YOU TO START DOING STUNTS. BOULDERING IS ALSO VERY SIMPLE, ESPECIALLY IF DONE INDOORS. YOU COULD TRY SWIMMING OR PLANNING A SIMPLE WORKOUT AT THE GYM.

Okay, now we have a game plan! Remember, not everything has to be perfect; you just need to work on making it as straightforward as possible. Let's try to plan for the next two weeks and see how it goes.

FOR THE NEXT TWO WEEKS, I WILL FOCUS ON THE FOLLOWING ACTIVITY (I.E., RUNNING, CLIMBING, CYCLING, YOGA):

_____

_____

_____

_____

_____

_____

MY BACKUP ACTIVITY FOR WHEN I FEEL LESS MOTIVATED WILL BE:

_____

_____

_____

_____

_____

_____

Depending on how many days per week you plan to exercise, fill in the following schedule accordingly. This form allows you to plan up to five days per week of exercising. Usually, three days per week is a good starting point.

EXAMPLE: DAY 1: <u>OCT. 10</u> FROM <u>5 P.M.</u> TO <u>6 P.M.</u>

WEEK 1

DAY 1:_____FROM_____TO_____
DAY 2:_____FROM_____TO_____
DAY 3:_____FROM_____TO_____
DAY 4:_____FROM_____TO_____
DAY 5:_____FROM_____TO_____

WEEK 2

DAY 1:_____FROM_____TO_____
DAY 2:_____FROM_____TO_____
DAY 3:_____FROM_____TO_____
DAY 4:_____FROM_____TO_____
DAY 5:_____FROM_____TO_____

Last but not least, let's talk about **rewards**!

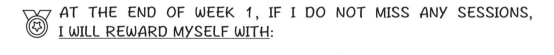 AT THE END OF WEEK 1, IF I DO NOT MISS ANY SESSIONS, I WILL REWARD MYSELF WITH:

_____

AT THE END OF WEEK 2, IF I DO NOT MISS ANY SESSIONS, I WILL REWARD MYSELF WITH:

_____

The rest of the chapter is dedicated to tracking your activity, re-assessing your barriers, and planning as you proceed with the training sessions.

WEEK 1 - ACTIVITY TRACKING

DAY 1

DID YOU DO THE SESSION?

☐ YES ☐ NO

DID YOU PREPARE EVERYTHING UPFRONT?

☐ YES ☐ NO

(CONTINUE IF YOU DID THE SESSION)
HOW LONG WAS THE SESSION?

HOW ENJOYABLE WAS IT?

WHAT ACTIVITIES DID YOU DO?

😃 🙂 😐 🙁 ☹️

DAY 2

DID YOU DO THE SESSION?

☐ YES ☐ NO

DID YOU PREPARE EVERYTHING UPFRONT?

☐ YES ☐ NO

(CONTINUE IF YOU DID THE SESSION)
HOW LONG WAS THE SESSION?

HOW ENJOYABLE WAS IT?

WHAT ACTIVITIES DID YOU DO?

😃 🙂 😐 🙁 ☹️

DAY 3

DID YOU DO THE SESSION?
☐ YES ☐ NO

DID YOU PREPARE EVERYTHING UPFRONT?
☐ YES ☐ NO

(CONTINUE IF YOU DID THE SESSION)
HOW LONG WAS THE SESSION?

HOW ENJOYABLE WAS IT?

😄 🙂 😐 🙁 ☹️

_____

WHAT ACTIVITIES DID YOU DO?

_____

_____

_____

DAY 4

DID YOU DO THE SESSION?
☐ YES ☐ NO

DID YOU PREPARE EVERYTHING UPFRONT?
☐ YES ☐ NO

(CONTINUE IF YOU DID THE SESSION)
HOW LONG WAS THE SESSION?

HOW ENJOYABLE WAS IT?

😄 🙂 😐 🙁 ☹️

_____

WHAT ACTIVITIES DID YOU DO?

_____

_____

_____

DAY 5

DID YOU DO THE SESSION?
☐ YES ☐ NO

DID YOU PREPARE EVERYTHING UPFRONT?
☐ YES ☐ NO

(CONTINUE IF YOU DID THE SESSION)
HOW LONG WAS THE SESSION?

HOW ENJOYABLE WAS IT?

😄 🙂 😐 🙁 ☹️

_____

WHAT ACTIVITIES DID YOU DO?

_____

_____

_____

WEEK 1 - SUMMARY AND RE-PLANNING

HOW MANY SESSIONS DID YOU DO DURING THE FIRST WEEK?

HOW MANY SESSIONS DID YOU SKIP DURING THE FIRST WEEK?

IF YOU SKIPPED ANY SESSIONS, WHY DID YOU SKIP THEM?

_____

_____

_____

_____

_____

DID YOU FACE ANY OF THE EXPECTED BARRIERS? IF YES, DESCRIBE THEM:

_____

_____

_____

_____

_____

DID YOU FACE ANY UNEXPECTED BARRIERS? IF YES, DESCRIBE THEM:

_____

_____

_____

_____

_____

DID YOUR PLAN TO TEAR DOWN THE EXPECTED BARRIERS WORK? IF NOT, OR IF IT WORKED ONLY PARTIALLY, USE THIS SPACE TO REVISE YOUR PLAN. THINK ABOUT WHAT DIDN'T WORK WELL AND WHAT YOU COULD DO DIFFERENTLY. ALSO, IF YOU HAVE FOUND OTHER UNEXPECTED BARRIERS, THINK ABOUT A PLAN TO TEAR THEM DOWN, TOO!

THE FIRST WEEKS ARE ALWAYS THE HARDEST. MOVING FROM PLANNING TO ACTING IS ALWAYS CHALLENGING, ESPECIALLY IF OUR ADHD BRAIN DECIDES TO GET IN OUR WAY. DON'T BE DISCOURAGED. THIS IS AN ITERATIVE LEARNING EXERCISE WHERE WE LEARN MORE ABOUT OURSELVES AND HOW TO OVERCOME OUR LIMITS.

WEEK 2 - ACTIVITY TRACKING

DAY 1

DID YOU DO THE SESSION?
☐ YES   ☐ NO

DID YOU PREPARE EVERYTHING UPFRONT?
☐ YES   ☐ NO

(CONTINUE IF YOU DID THE SESSION)

HOW LONG WAS THE SESSION?

_____

HOW ENJOYABLE WAS IT?

😀 🙂 😐 🙁 ☹️

WHAT ACTIVITIES DID YOU DO?

_____

_____

_____

_____

_____

DAY 2

DID YOU DO THE SESSION?
☐ YES   ☐ NO

DID YOU PREPARE EVERYTHING UPFRONT?
☐ YES   ☐ NO

(CONTINUE IF YOU DID THE SESSION)

HOW LONG WAS THE SESSION?

_____

HOW ENJOYABLE WAS IT?

😀 🙂 😐 🙁 ☹️

WHAT ACTIVITIES DID YOU DO?

_____

_____

_____

_____

_____

_____

DAY 3

DID YOU DO THE SESSION?
☐ YES   ☐ NO

DID YOU PREPARE EVERYTHING UPFRONT?
☐ YES   ☐ NO

(CONTINUE IF YOU DID THE SESSION)
HOW LONG WAS THE SESSION?

_____

HOW ENJOYABLE WAS IT?

😃 🙂 😐 🙁 ☹️

WHAT ACTIVITIES DID YOU DO?

_____

_____

_____

DAY 4

DID YOU DO THE SESSION?
☐ YES   ☐ NO

DID YOU PREPARE EVERYTHING UPFRONT?
☐ YES   ☐ NO

(CONTINUE IF YOU DID THE SESSION)
HOW LONG WAS THE SESSION?

_____

HOW ENJOYABLE WAS IT?

😃 🙂 😐 🙁 ☹️

WHAT ACTIVITIES DID YOU DO?

_____

_____

_____

DAY 5

DID YOU DO THE SESSION?
☐ YES   ☐ NO

DID YOU PREPARE EVERYTHING UPFRONT?
☐ YES   ☐ NO

(CONTINUE IF YOU DID THE SESSION)
HOW LONG WAS THE SESSION?

_____

HOW ENJOYABLE WAS IT?

😃 🙂 😐 🙁 ☹️

WHAT ACTIVITIES DID YOU DO?

_____

_____

_____

WEEK 2 - SUMMARY AND RE-PLANNING

HOW MANY SESSIONS DID YOU DO DURING THE FIRST WEEK?

HOW MANY SESSIONS DID YOU SKIP DURING THE FIRST WEEK?

_____

IF YOU SKIPPED ANY SESSIONS, WHY DID YOU SKIP THEM?

_____

_____

_____

_____

_____

DID YOU FACE ANY OF THE EXPECTED BARRIERS? IF YES, DESCRIBE THEM:

_____

_____

_____

_____

_____

DID YOU FACE ANY UNEXPECTED BARRIERS? IF YES, DESCRIBE THEM:

_____

_____

_____

_____

_____

DID YOUR PLAN TO TEAR DOWN THE EXPECTED BARRIERS WORK? IF NOT, OR IF IT WORKED ONLY PARTIALLY, USE THIS SPACE TO REVISE YOUR PLAN. THINK ABOUT WHAT DIDN'T WORK WELL AND WHAT YOU COULD DO DIFFERENTLY. ALSO, IF YOU HAVE FOUND OTHER UNEXPECTED BARRIERS, THINK ABOUT A PLAN TO TEAR THEM DOWN, TOO!

After two weeks of training, you are probably starting to get the hang of the process. Especially if you are committing to a regular training regime for the first time, you will soon realize that the number of unexpected barriers will progressively decrease. In addition, with this iterative process, you will slowly become conscious of some challenges that have always been bothering you and come up with the best plan to overcome them.

The hard truth is that some of these barriers will always be there, while others will become more manageable with good planning and thinking.

If, after two weeks, you feel like this process has been helpful, I've prepared a set of online resources you can download and print to plan your next weeks. There is no shame in realizing this approach doesn't work for you, however. It worked well for many of my clients and me, but in some cases, we had to take a different, personalized approach.

If you want to progress with this method, you can download and print the online resources. The link and QR code are available on page 142.

CHAPTER 3

GOAL-SETTING AND GOAL-GETTING

*T*wo of the most constant challenges for people with ADHD are goal-setting and goal-getting.

GOAL-SETTING INVOLVES PLANNING FOR THE FUTURE, UNDERSTANDING WHICH GOALS ARE MEANINGFUL FOR US, AND PRIORITIZING THEM.

Goal-getting is about staying focused on these goals and not getting distracted by other stuff or derailed by barriers and obstacles we will encounter in the process of achieving those goals.

In my career, I've never met a woman who has ADHD and doesn't struggle with goal-setting and goal-getting; this is totally normal due to how our ADHD brain is wired.

If you think about it, this is not easy for anyone; otherwise, we would live in this utopian society where everyone consistently achieved all their goals. The reality is much different.

Human beings always aspire to something more; we constantly chase distant objectives. This is already difficult for women who do not have ADHD.

No one teaches us how to set goals, and there are infinite ways to achieve them.

For us, it is incredibly challenging; basically, 90% of ADHD symptoms will get in our way.

If you think about it, setting and achieving a goal requires planning, prioritizing, and sustaining an effort toward the objective. Also, we have to stay focused and motivated throughout the process. If it sounds complicated, that's because it is! ADHD affects all these skills at different levels. We are more likely to set goals impulsively and take on more than we can realistically handle.

As if that wasn't enough, internal obstacles often add to the problem. The sense of shame and dissatisfaction in finding even the simplest tasks harder than necessary can create additional barriers that prevent us from achieving our goals. Perhaps this is why we often find it easier to accomplish things we had not even planned to do.

So, why try at all? Why spend all this time and energy dealing with the stress and shame that comes with trying to achieve goals we will almost certainly fail to achieve? Well, most importantly, we must stick with setting up goals. Objectives are essential for progress and change for the better. I am not talking only about work but about life. Plans give people a reason to jump off the bed in the morning and are essential to fight boredom and build self-confidence. Achieving them can be stressful and painful, but a life without goals would be meaningless and empty. So, we must keep trying!

For some women, it might be more effective to focus on putting systems in place to support what we want to accomplish than to set goals, but according to Alan R. Graham, an ADHD coach (Ph.D., ACP Consultants), there is another option.

This methodology has proved helpful for countless people, and I often suggest it to my clients.

In his opinion, the key is planning. We should allocate enough time upfront to create a plan for achieving our goals, increasing the possibility of being successful.

The question is, how do we do that?

When Alan coaches a person in goal-setting, he asks the following questions:

- What's the goal?
- Why that goal?
- What are the benefits of doing it?
- What are the benefits of not doing it?
- What is the cost of doing it?
- What is the cost of not doing it?
- What **obstacles** are we likely to face, and how will we handle them?

WHAT'S THE GOAL?

I've noticed that the first question is tricky for many people because sometimes we think we have the goal clear in our minds when this is not actually the case. However, a clear and well-defined goal is paramount for success. Let me give you a few examples:

X Inaccurate goal: *"I want to finish that term paper."*

✓ Accurate goal: *"Performance goal: I want to finish Modern English term paper by 2023/12/12; it has to be at least 5,000 words."*

X Inaccurate goal: *"I want to get better at playing guitar."*

✓ Accurate goal: *"Self-Improvement goal: I want to learn how to use vibrato technique with guitar and perform Blur's 'Tender' song."*

As you can see, accuracy is everything; otherwise, you won't even understand if or when you have achieved your goal.

WHY THAT GOAL?

We ask this question to ourselves to understand how motivated we are to achieve our goals.

Think about motivation as the fuel we use to reach our goals. If we don't have enough fuel in our tanks, we will stop midway and retire from the race. We need enough motivation to deal with obstacles as they come, and for this reason, we want to be sure we are choosing a goal that either we care about or must do.

BENEFITS VS. COST

This section is about understanding the benefits of achieving a particular goal and comparing them with the costs. When we talk about the costs, we don't mean monetary costs only. Instead, this is about your time, the effort you must put into it, and the sacrifices you must make.

On the flip side, we want to understand what it would cost us to not do it. What are the implications if we don't work toward achieving a particular goal? Are we losing any opportunities? What will be the impact on our life or the people around us? Also, are there any benefits to not doing it? For instance, it might be the case that through sacrificing a specific goal, we can work toward a more important one.

With this approach, we can weigh the pros and cons of doing and not doing a particular thing. The concept we are applying is called "mental contrasting":

> *"Mental contrasting is a self-regulation strategy that is required for strong goal commitment. In mental contrasting, individuals firstly imagine a desired future or health goal that contrasts with the reality preceding the goal state, which after reflection is viewed as an obstacle. Mentally contrasting a positive future with reality enables individuals to translate positive attitudes and high efficacy into strong goal commitment."* (Cross A., 2016)

Research shows that mental contrasting is incredibly effective in helping people with ADHD to set and stick to goals. It helps us triage our goals and understand what is worth it and what we can postpone.

HOW TO DEAL WITH OBSTACLES

This last section is about how to deal with the barriers we might encounter. This will prepare our brains for situations where we need to decide how to deal with them. You want to think, "If this happens," then "I will do this," and consider as many likely scenarios as possible.

The work we will do is like a chess player thinking 10 moves ahead of her opponent; you are doing the same thing, not on a chess board but in reality.

Obviously, we won't be able to see all the potential obstacles from the beginning. Still, we can see some of them, and figuring out how to deal with some barriers will save our executive function resources for the ones we can't predict. Through this process, we can create strong, highly motivating goals and set up strategies to deal with the barriers we expect to find in our path.

I've personally found this method beneficial, and I often use it in my daily life. Also, it resonated well with many of the people I've coached. Shall we give it a try?

Let's work toward a single goal and see how it goes!

WHAT'S THE GOAL?

_____

_____

WHY THAT GOAL?

_____

_____

BENEFITS OF DOING	BENEFITS OF NOT DOING
COST OF DOING	COST OF NOT DOING

Barriers that we are likely to face:

BARRIER	STRATEGY TO HANDLE IT

We want to be sure to track our progress, since most people with ADHD need an extra level of accountability to see some tasks through to their end.

The idea of tracking our progress is based on Pearson's law: "When a performance is measured and reported, it improves exponentially." We want to take advantage of this and bring accountability to the game.

One way to do it is with an **accountability buddy**; someone we can meet, talk to, and share our progress with. An accountability buddy can help us navigate those challenges, offering a different perspective or simply cheering us on.

Finding an accountability buddy might not be simple for everyone, but here are some options you might consider:

Ask your partner. This doesn't work for me and some of my clients, while for other women this is a perfect solution. I always fight with my husband every time he monitors my progress, but just because this happens to me and some couples doesn't mean it won't work for you. So, give it a try before giving up on this option.

- Ask a friend who may be willing to help.

- Ask your family members.

- Post on Facebook or other social media to see if there is anyone in your network who may be interested.

- Join a free mastermind group. These are groups of peers who meet to give each other advice and support.

- Join a dedicated program, like the "Accelerated Momentum Program" by Dr. Benjamin Hardy.

Some of us might not desire to share our goals or involve others, which is fine. The important thing is fostering accountability. If you don't want to work with an accountability buddy, you could decide instead to have your own daily and weekly check-ins.

With this approach, you will report your progress on your goal with a fixed frequency. For instance, let's say you want to learn guitar and you decide to run weekly check-ins. Every week, you will set an objective, i.e., play the guitar for at least three hours.

During your weekly check-in, you will report on your week's performance. I suggest doing this in writing since it helps to visualize the progress. Also, to keep your motivation high, you can set up small weekly rewards and penalties based on your performance.

If you have no idea how to structure your check-ins, I've included an essential structure for the first month below. Also, I suggest looking into the time management chapter before committing to your goals. It should significantly help you put your goals on a schedule.

One last thing: If you like this method and you want to keep having your weekly check-ins after the first month, you can use the online resources at page 13 and 14.

(EXAMPLE) WEEK 1 CHECK-IN

WEEKLY OBJECTIVE: ACHIEVED:

Play the guitar for at least three hours   ☑ YES
_____   ☐ NO

💵 <u>FINE</u> TO BE APPLIED IF NOT ACHIEVED:

Remove $25 from weekly drinks budget
_____

🏅 WEEKLY <u>REWARD</u>, IF ACHIEVED:

Order take-away from my favorite Italian place
_____

WEEK 1 CHECK-IN

WEEKLY OBJECTIVE: ACHIEVED:

_____   ☐ YES
_____   ☐ NO

💵 <u>FINE</u> TO BE APPLIED IF NOT ACHIEVED:

_____
_____

🏅 WEEKLY <u>REWARD</u>, IF ACHIEVED:

_____
_____

WEEK 2 CHECK-IN

WEEKLY OBJECTIVE: ACHIEVED:

_____   ☐ YES

_____   ☐ NO

💵 <u>FINE</u> TO BE APPLIED IF NOT ACHIEVED:

_____

_____

🏅 WEEKLY <u>REWARD</u>, IF ACHIEVED:

_____

_____

WEEK 3 CHECK-IN

WEEKLY OBJECTIVE: ACHIEVED:

_____   ☐ YES

_____   ☐ NO

💵 <u>FINE</u> TO BE APPLIED IF NOT ACHIEVED:

_____

_____

🏅 WEEKLY <u>REWARD</u>, IF ACHIEVED:

_____

_____

CHAPTER 4

TIME MANAGEMENT

Struggling with time management is more common than you think. Many people, especially those diagnosed with ADHD, often find it challenging to make the most of their day and stick to a productive schedule.

I've always struggled with planning, a common trait in many women with ADHD. However, we all must make an effort in this area. We don't need our nights stretching until 4 a.m., because getting things done is terrific but taking care of ourselves matters, too!

Schedules can be seen as constrictive, blocking the freedom to do what we want. But when you need one and don't have it in place, that lack of planning may come back to bite you! Time management is essential for success, but sometimes our brains rebel against creating a plan; we crave spontaneity instead. Let's face it. Most of us, by the time we sit down and make a schedule, really need one, but it is already too late!

A schedule is an incredibly useful resource if we embrace it, not something to be feared. It's just a tool that can help us make the most of our time and reach our goals.

A well-planned schedule gives us control over our daily lives while allowing us the flexibility to deal with unexpected events without sacrificing progress toward larger goals. It creates a framework that enables us to conquer everyday tasks and surpass obstacles; the perfect balance of organization and adaptability.

Okay, this sounds amazing, but how do we even begin to create a schedule? A lot of us aren't confident that we can even estimate how long a task is going to take. In this situation, how can we possibly create a reliable plan? Also, are we not setting ourselves up for failure? If we don't have a schedule, everything we do is a success, but if we cannot follow a schedule, everything is a failure.

A lot of questions, a lot of doubts. Let's keep it simple. I like to think there is no such thing as failure. There is "success," and there is "learning." Obviously, easier said than done.

People with ADHD have a more extensive collection of "failures" than others, and in most cases, a certain degree of shame is involved. So it's natural to be hesitant when pursuing something new. It takes courage and resilience to rise above the fear of potential failure.

Also, our sense of time is pretty lousy. What we think will take 10 minutes will never take 10 minutes. Basically, if we jump into weekly planning using our "old" sense of time, we are likely to make mistakes. We don't want that; we don't want to feel overwhelmed and like we have too much on our plate. Let's work on this step by step.

STEP 1: FIND OUT HOW LONG THINGS TAKE YOU

Instead of jumping head-first into building a schedule, let's spend a week doing some research on ourselves. Take your standard to-do list, with all your tasks written down, and try to guess how long each item on that list will take you to complete.

For example, one of your tasks says "prepare breakfast." You estimate it will take 30 minutes of your time. When you start the task, you will also start a count-up timer to keep track of how long it takes you. Write down how long it took. When estimating, remember that things often require prep time and clean-up time. We often neglect to consider additional time investments when assessing our tasks; however, these extra minutes can make or break a timeline. We must recognize and plan for them accordingly!

Using the space below, report at least 15 tasks you usually do in a week with your time estimation to perform them and how much time you actually spent to complete them.

....

TASK: _____

🕐 ESTIMATED TIME REQUIRED: ⏱ ACTUAL TIME REQUIRED:

_____ _____

....

TASK: _____

🕐 ESTIMATED TIME REQUIRED: ⏱ ACTUAL TIME REQUIRED:

_____ _____

....

TASK: _____

🕐 ESTIMATED TIME REQUIRED: ⏱ ACTUAL TIME REQUIRED:

_____ _____

....

TASK: _____

🕐 ESTIMATED TIME REQUIRED: ⏱ ACTUAL TIME REQUIRED:

_____ _____

....

TASK:

🕐 ESTIMATED TIME REQUIRED: ⏱ ACTUAL TIME REQUIRED:

TASK:

🕐 ESTIMATED TIME REQUIRED: ⏱ ACTUAL TIME REQUIRED:

TASK:

🕐 ESTIMATED TIME REQUIRED: ⏱ ACTUAL TIME REQUIRED:

TASK:

🕐 ESTIMATED TIME REQUIRED: ⏱ ACTUAL TIME REQUIRED:

....

TASK: _____

🕐 ESTIMATED TIME REQUIRED: ⏱ ACTUAL TIME REQUIRED:

_____   _____

....

TASK: _____

🕐 ESTIMATED TIME REQUIRED: ⏱ ACTUAL TIME REQUIRED:

_____   _____

....

TASK: _____

🕐 ESTIMATED TIME REQUIRED: ⏱ ACTUAL TIME REQUIRED:

_____   _____

....

TASK: _____

🕐 ESTIMATED TIME REQUIRED: ⏱ ACTUAL TIME REQUIRED:

_____   _____

....

....

TASK: _____

🕐 ESTIMATED TIME REQUIRED: ⏱ ACTUAL TIME REQUIRED:

_____   _____

....

TASK: _____

🕐 ESTIMATED TIME REQUIRED: ⏱ ACTUAL TIME REQUIRED:

_____   _____

....

TASK: _____

🕐 ESTIMATED TIME REQUIRED: ⏱ ACTUAL TIME REQUIRED:

_____   _____

....

TASK: _____

🕐 ESTIMATED TIME REQUIRED: ⏱ ACTUAL TIME REQUIRED:

_____   _____

....

When I first attempted this exercise, I couldn't manage to time myself consistently, but I started to recognize a **pattern**. I was wildly off the mark, underestimating how long a task would take me if I didn't have much prior experience with the job or if it required multiple steps.

Consider doing the same thing and reporting your considerations in the space below. Sometimes this process is eye-opening and can help improve how we estimate the size of our tasks.

AFTER TIMING MYSELF FOR A WEEK, I'VE NOTICED THE FOLLOWING PATTERNS:

STEP 2: CREATE YOUR SCHEDULE

Now that we understand how our sense of time can be distorted, let's make the most out of this knowledge by creating an effective schedule. How will we use what we've learned to maximize efficiency? Let's find out!

Often, people ask what the best app or calendar is to keep their schedules. The answer is simple: the one you like. I like Google Calendar, but even a simple notebook would do the job. The important thing is to use only one and not have multiple calendars around. Using various tools simultaneously will add new issues, like ensuring that everything is in sync, and you might find yourself with multiple calendars that may be outdated.

Now, the big question is, "What do I put on my schedule?"

The first thing to do is include your existing commitments, appointments, deadlines, due dates, and anything you know is coming up. If you have big projects coming up, I strongly suggest making your calendar very loud about it.

For instance, let's say you have your wedding in 12 weeks. Instead of flagging only the wedding date, I would put weekly reminders, like "wedding is in seven weeks" or "wedding is in six weeks." This helps you keep the event in mind and avoid that surprise effect of "Crap! The wedding is in 10 days!"

There are other items in your schedule that you could classify as "IBNU" (Important But Not Urgent). These are meaningful things for you, even if they are not linked to any deadline. For IBNU, we will use block scheduling, which is blocking time for yourself on your schedule for things you never do because they are not urgent. Based on your estimations in Step 1, remember to give yourself more time than you think you might need. Also, leave some time free before and after any activity. Transitions can be challenging for some of us, as we struggle to shift our focus from one task to another.

The most common question I get from clients at this point is, "Okay, but what if I don't have time for everything?"

You have to understand that there are so many paradoxes when we talk about productivity, and probably the most important one is "less is more."

To make significant progress on a single task or project, it is essential to recognize when delegation and pushing back are the best options. Rather than trying to multitask, focus on moving one goal forward efficiently with clear limits set in place.

It is tough to delegate, say no to things, and get rid of them, but I think the cost of not doing it is so high that it is worth the price. I remember when, years ago, I was constantly overwhelmed, taking on so much more than I probably should have, mainly to make people happy. This behavior was just unhealthy, and I was falling short as well as apart. I got tired of not getting things done, so I've started letting go of some stuff. To understand what I wanted to keep, I asked myself, "What do I want to grow?"

For instance, you might decide that your focus should be on your morning yoga and preparing for an important meeting. If that's the case, you should start making space to allow enough time for these activities.

I've created a daily calendar and a weekly planner for the internet resources that you may use to make your own agenda. You can find them on pages 18, 19, and 20 of the online resources if you want to give them a try.

STEP 3: STICK TO YOUR SCHEDULE

As an ADHDer, one of the hardest things for us is to stick to a schedule; many things can go wrong even if we correctly estimate all the tasks.

Let's look at some of the more common problems that can arise when we try to stick to a schedule.

Breaking out of hyperfocus: According to Brandon K. Ashinoff, a researcher at Columbia University:

> *"Hyperfocus is a state of intense concentration where you lose track of time, you really enjoy what you're doing, and you seem to be better at that than whatever it is you're doing. Now, if you're playing a video game, you're really good at playing that video game. If you're playing a sport, you get really good at playing that sport, that sort of thing. This is weird in the context of ADHD because it's actually too much attention. You're focused so intently on something; no other information gets into your brain essentially."*

Sometimes it just happens that we enter hyperfocus mode, and even if a task should take a couple of hours, we could spend six hours on it without even noticing. Hyperfocus can provide us with an array of advantages if managed correctly, but it's not without its drawbacks. Unlocking this superpower requires careful balancing. If we don't pace ourselves in hyperfocus mode, we could quickly burn all our energies on a single task and lose track of all the rest.

To avoid the hyperfocus trap, we can adopt a technique called "**Leaving yourself a trail of crumbs.**"

This approach is simple. While you are performing a task, write what you did and the following one or two things you would do if you continued working on it. This will give you a structured approach and reduce the risk of losing control and falling down the rabbit hole.

Fight the "I don't want to do it" feeling: Sometimes, we are not in the mood to do something, even if we should. The easiest way to find motivation is to create **accountability**—tell somebody! If you want to keep up with your schedule and not stay awake until late, you sometimes have to do things when you don't want to. In these cases, accountability can help a lot to stay on track.

What if I'm excited about something else? Having ADHD means our brains run fast; we have many ideas and the urge to jump on them immediately. One way to deal with that is by adopting the "**parking lot**" approach.

The idea is to jot down inspiration instantly with this method and quickly resume the task at hand. This approach will allow us to keep focus and never let a brilliant thought pass by.

Our "parking lot" can be a simple notebook. The most important thing to remember is to time-box this activity and not risk spending hours on it.

Is there a good time to "ride the wave?" Sometimes we are just inspired to do something that we usually wouldn't do, like having the urge to clean the patio or organize the documents we have around. Is it reasonable to ride the wave and do these things since we are inspired, or shall we stick to the schedule? It depends on the context. Ideally, especially in the beginning, you want to stick to your calendar. Once you get more comfortable with following a schedule, you can start thinking about adapting it and see if you can make space for these spontaneous waves of productivity.

Check your schedule: You should consider your schedule to be your GPS. It will guide you in what you are trying to do and will lead you where you want to go. If we go with this analogy and you are driving somewhere, would you put your GPS in the trunk after you arrive at your destination? Obviously not. Your schedule is the same; you must have it with you and check on it for directions.

This concludes the time management chapter. I hope you found the techniques presented useful.

CHAPTER 5

IMPROVE YOUR WORKING MEMORY

*A*lthough ADHD is most commonly recognized for causing attention deficits, many don't realize that it likely affects working memory, too. Working memory issues are thought to be a hidden symptom of this disorder—one shrouded in mystery yet essential to understanding the condition better.

Our working memory is an incredible feat of neural engineering, allowing us to take in and manipulate information for short periods. Furthermore, it provides the foundation upon which we can reason and problem-solve with remarkable efficiency. Unfortunately, this executive function is often impaired with ADHD.

If we compare ourselves to computers, the working memory is our RAM. It is a place where we store information that we are actively using.

We use our working memory in many situations, even if we don't realize it. We use short-time memory to

- remember a telephone number while we are looking for a pen and paper to write it down,
- do some math in our heads,
- remember what we just read,

… and tons of other stuff!

Working memory is a scarce resource; we can typically keep in mind just a fraction of what we would like, and the information stored quickly disappears if we don't actively focus on it.

This is usually not a problem; most of the information in our short-term memory will not serve us in the long term.

The main challenge is that we have less "space" in our working memory than neurotypical people. This issue is further amplified when it comes to keeping verbal/auditory information in memory. Let me give you an example:

Imagine that in a school class, there are two students. One is an ADHD person, and the other is neurotypical. The ADHD student can keep only three pieces of information in working memory, while the neurotypical student can hold four.

The teacher asks a question followed by three possible answers. The neurotypical student can remember the question plus the three possible answers, filling all four slots. The only challenge the neurotypical person faces is knowing the correct answer to the question.

Unfortunately, the ADHD student has limited capacity and can hold only the question and two possible answers. When the teacher starts to read the third possible answer, the ADHD student forgets the original question.

It stands to reason that there may be other elements at play regarding our inability to retain certain information; factors such as attention and focus could significantly impact how long we can keep hold of the data in question. Still, this is an excellent example of our daily challenges. None of this happens because we are not smart enough or because we aren't trying; this is just how the ADHD brain works.

Saving working memory consumption is one of the main reasons why many coaches suggest using lists and planners. These tools can save our "working memory slots" for information we actively use instead of filling it up with information we don't want to lose.

It is important to notice that a global brain deficit does not cause this issue. Instead, this problem is localized in three main areas and connections between those areas. Furthermore, we can act indirectly on these areas to improve their efficiency and our working memory.

Torken Klingberg, professor of cognitive neuroscience at the Karolinska Institute in Stockholm, Sweden, developed a short-memory training program in 2008. He used specifically designed computer games to help the test subjects increase their working memory capacity. The results were impressive: After five weeks of gaming, the volunteers increased their working memory capacity by between 15% and 22%.

The idea behind this working program is simple: Working memory is like a muscle, and it can be trained.

Suppose we observe this from a neuroscientist's point of view. In that case, we would see that after the training program, some changes are visible in the three brain areas responsible for working memory management. Specifically, post-training, the connectivity between those regions is more robust, and they act less like a bottleneck than before. Some of you may be wondering, "Okay, this is cool, but does improving working memory through games translate into results in real life?" Yes, Professor Klingberg proved that the detected working memory improvement translates directly into a stronger ability to memorize and execute instructions.

So, do we need specific video games to train our working memory? Not necessarily; there are a lot of simple exercises that can help with it and that work similarly.

We want to create a daily routine that is challenging enough to push our working memory to its limits. Below, you will find a set of exercises. You can mix them as you prefer or create your own, modifying the activities provided. Please remember not to take notes. You want to perform these exercises using only your mind. Your objective is to challenge your brain for 30 consecutive minutes each day for at least two weeks.

Depending on your execution speed, you might need to repeat the same type of exercises multiple times, but be sure to vary them slightly.

The results vary from person to person, and age is one factor that influences how much we can improve our working memory.

The brains of younger women demonstrate more flexibility and the ability to adapt more quickly to stimuli. Older women will see slower results. Unfortunately, I was among this second group when I started training my working memory. I probably struggled a bit more, but I've still seen some good results in the end.

Exercise type 1) **Playing With Numbers**

- Start with 20 and count backward by twos.
- Start with 30 and count backward by threes.
- Start with 40 and count backward by fours.
- Start with 50 and count backward by fives.
- Start with 30 and count backward by sixes.
- Start with 35 and count backward by sevens.
- Start with 40 and count backward by eights.
- Start with 45 and count backward by nines.
- Start with 75 and count backward by fives.
- Start with 81 and count backward by threes.
- Start with 84 and count backward by sevens.
- Start with 90 and count backward by twos.

Exercise type 2) **Playing With Days and Months**

- Start with Tuesday and say every other day.
- Start with Saturday and say the days of the week backward.
- Start with Thursday and say every other day.
- Start with March and say every other month.
- Start with June and say the months backward.
- Say the last seven months of the year.
- Say the months backward starting from October.
- What is the eighth month of the year? Spell it backward.
- What is the third month of the year? Spell it backward.
- What is the seventh month of the year? Spell it backward.
- What is the third day of the week? Spell it backward.
- What is the fifth day of the week? Spell it backward.

Exercise type 3) **Playing With the Alphabet**

- What is the 10th letter of the alphabet?
- What is the 15th letter of the alphabet?
- What letter comes before G in the alphabet?
- What letter comes before P in the alphabet?
- What letter comes before M in the alphabet?
- What letter comes before L?
- Say the alphabet backward, starting from L.
- What letter comes before K in the alphabet?
- What are the last five letters of the alphabet?
- What is the 17th letter of the alphabet?
- Say the alphabet but replace every vowel with incremental numbers, starting from 1.
- Say the alphabet backward, replacing every vowel with incremental numbers, starting from 1.

Exercise type 4) **Rhymes**

- Find a word that rhymes with "rat," now try to spell it backward.
- Find a word that rhymes with "scar," now try to spell it backward.
- Find a word that rhymes with "lips," now try to spell it backward.
- Find a word that rhymes with "skate," now try to spell it backward.
- Find a word that rhymes with "house," now try to spell it backward.
- Find a word that rhymes with "red," now try to spell it backward.
- Find a word that rhymes with "rat," now try to spell it backward, replacing every vowel with incremental numbers. Start from 1.
- Find a word that rhymes with "scar," now try to spell it backward, replacing every vowel with incremental numbers. Start from 7.
- Find a word that rhymes with "lips," now try to spell it backward, replacing every vowel with incremental numbers. Start from 2.
- Find a word that rhymes with "skate," now try to spell it backward, replacing every vowel with incremental numbers. Start from 3.
- Find a word that rhymes with "house," now try to spell it backward.
- Find a word that rhymes with "red," now try to spell it backward, replacing every vowel with incremental numbers. Start from 99.

Exercise type 5) **Opposites**

- Find the opposite of "last," now try to spell it backward.
- Find the opposite of "tall," now try to spell it backward.
- Find the opposite of "sad," now try to spell it backward.
- Find the opposite of "below," now try to spell it backward.
- Find the opposite of "east," now try to spell it backward.
- Find the opposite of "light," now try to spell it backward.

Exercise type 6) **Pick a...**

- Pick a color, now try to spell it backward.
- Pick a sport, now try to spell it backward.
- Pick a movie title, now try to spell it backward.
- Pick a vegetable, now try to spell it backward.
- Pick a song, now try to spell it backward.
- Pick a job, now try to spell it backward.
- Pick a celebrity's last name, now try to spell it backward.
- Pick an animal, now try to spell it backward.
- Pick a number, now try to spell it backward.
- Pick a city, now try to spell it backward.
- Pick a state, now try to spell it backward.
- Pick a flower, now try to spell it backward.

If you struggle to perform these tasks, don't worry, this is normal. Our brain is not wired to perform these exercises efficiently; they are purposely designed to push it to its limits.

If you are among the few who find these tasks too easy, you can increase the difficulty by juggling multiple things in parallel. Grab a deck of cards. While performing the above exercises, you could sort the deck into suits and then put each suit of cards into numerical order.

CHAPTER 6
HOW TO SAY "NO"

*A*re you feeling stuck in a never-ending cycle of stress and fatigue? You're not alone—many women experience this same pressure each day.

Growing up, I suffered a lot from this problem, and the fact that I could not stop always saying "yes" did not help.

I later realized that this wasn't my problem only; women with ADHD often find themselves saying "yes" to virtually everything. Studies suggest that this tendency could arise from biological differences in the brain or be based on environmental influences such as societal pressures. Among the most common reasons for this widespread trait, you can find

- people pleasing
- impulsivity
- enthusiasm
- not valuing your time enough
- low self-esteem
- poor planning and estimation skills
- inability to prioritize
- … and much, much more!

The problem is that being unable to say "no" creates a vicious circle. The more we take on, the more we increase our workload, and the more likely we are to fail. The more we fail, the more we feel ashamed. Then our self-esteem drops, and we value our time less. So, we take more!

Despite being just two letters, "No" can be surprisingly tricky for many of us to express. However, understanding when and how to decline gracefully is an invaluable skill when the opportunity presents itself.

Breaking free from an endless cycle of obligation and demand can be daunting, but the tips included in this chapter will give you the insight to set yourself on a better path. Learn how to say "no" confidently without fearing backlash or guilt.

DETERMINE WHEN YOU WILL SAY "YES"

Since our brains don't naturally prioritize well, it is imperative to externalize the decision process that leads to "yes" or "no."

How can we decide which commitments deserve our utmost attention and effort? We do it in advance with a straightforward approach.

Women with ADHD typically have problems making decisions in the heat of the moment because their executive function system doesn't perform well under pressure.

It is essential to notice that we can differentiate between the hot executive function system (HEFS) and the cool executive function system (CEFS).

HEFS makes decisions and prioritizes under pressure quickly, while CEFS makes decisions and prioritizes in advance.

HEFS is commonly impaired for people with ADHD, but CEFS typically works well.

We want to rely on our CEFS and prepare our list of priorities in advance. Also, we could build a list of anti-priorities, or things we won't say "yes" to because we learned from experience that they are unsuitable for achieving our goals and don't lead to happiness.

The main goal is to reduce the odds that our ADHD brain will decide, basing such decisions only on what we feel in the moment. Regarding pure prioritization, the techniques explained in the "Goal-Setting and Goal-Getting" and "Time Management" chapters are valid and can also be applied for this specific case.

In addition to what we've learned, I want to introduce the concept of **priorities** and **anti-priorities** to support your decision process.

We can break down priorities and anti-priorities into "short," "medium," and "long" term:

- **Short term:** These are DAILY priorities and anti-priorities.
- **Medium term:** These priorities and anti-priorities commonly refer to the WEEK or the MONTH.
- **Long term:** These usually are YEARLY priorities and anti-priorities.

We want to use a top-down approach, starting from the long-term priorities and defining what we care about and don't care about.

Let me give you an example. For this year, **my long-term priorities** were:

- Finish writing this book
- Learn to play tennis
- Create my website with some useful resources for people with ADHD

My **anti-priorities** were:

- Avoid being involved in other conferences. It takes too long to prepare them, and they are incredibly stressful.
- I've to stop picking up new gym activities. I'm already following enough classes.
- I go shopping for shoes only if I need them and don't waste my time. Also, I've to throw away an old pair first. I don't have any space left at home; shoes are everywhere!

Now it is your turn. In the next pages, list your top five long-term priorities and anti-priorities.

LONG-TERM PRIORITIES	LONG-TERM ANTI-PRIORITIES

Now that you have a clearer idea of your long-term priorities, let's define those for the week. In this case, for the medium-term priorities, we want to limit ourselves only to the three most important ones.

MEDIUM-TERM PRIORITIES	MEDIUM-TERM ANTI-PRIORITIES

Last, we want to define the priority for the day. Again, these will be short-term priorities and represent what we want to focus on tomorrow.

SHORT-TERM PRIORITIES	SHORT-TERM ANTI-PRIORITIES

This methodology for defining priorities is similar to setting a generic calendar. Based on what we have described in the tables above, we now know what we want and don't want to do. This method will help us say "no" to activities that could distract us from our priorities.

Before committing to a technique, I always suggest trying it for a short period and seeing if it works for you. For example, try using this method for two weeks, simply updating your daily priorities the night before or early in the morning so you can set them in mind for the day.

Likewise, you can edit the medium- and long-term priorities weekly based on the progress achieved and the natural change in priorities.

I have left two weeks of prioritization in the next pages, ready to be compiled.

If, after these two weeks, you have enjoyed this method and decide to continue using it, you can print pages 23 and 24 of the online resources to keep tracking your weekly priorities.

WEEK 1

MEDIUM-TERM PRIORITIES	MEDIUM-TERM ANTI-PRIORITIES

DAY: ___ /___ /___   SUNDAY

SHORT-TERM PRIORITIES	SHORT-TERM ANTI-PRIORITIES

DAY: __ / __ / __   MONDAY

SHORT-TERM PRIORITIES	SHORT-TERM ANTI-PRIORITIES

. . . .

DAY: __ / __ / __   TUESDAY

SHORT-TERM PRIORITIES	SHORT-TERM ANTI-PRIORITIES

DAY: ___ / ___ / ___   WEDNESDAY

SHORT-TERM PRIORITIES	SHORT-TERM ANTI-PRIORITIES

....

DAY: ___ / ___ / ___   THURSDAY

SHORT-TERM PRIORITIES	SHORT-TERM ANTI-PRIORITIES

DAY: ___ / ___ / ___   FRIDAY

SHORT-TERM PRIORITIES	SHORT-TERM ANTI-PRIORITIES

DAY: ___ / ___ / ___   SATURDAY

SHORT-TERM PRIORITIES	SHORT-TERM ANTI-PRIORITIES

MEDIUM-TERM PRIORITIES	MEDIUM-TERM ANTI-PRIORITIES

DAY: ___ / ___ / ___

SUNDAY

SHORT-TERM PRIORITIES	SHORT-TERM ANTI-PRIORITIES

DAY: ___ /___ /___   MONDAY

SHORT-TERM PRIORITIES	SHORT-TERM ANTI-PRIORITIES

DAY: ___ /___ /___   TUESDAY

SHORT-TERM PRIORITIES	SHORT-TERM ANTI-PRIORITIES

DAY: ___ /___ /___   WEDNESDAY

SHORT-TERM PRIORITIES	SHORT-TERM ANTI-PRIORITIES

....

DAY: ___ /___ /___   THURSDAY

SHORT-TERM PRIORITIES	SHORT-TERM ANTI-PRIORITIES

DAY: ___ /___ /___   FRIDAY

SHORT-TERM PRIORITIES	SHORT-TERM ANTI-PRIORITIES

DAY: ___ /___ /___   SATURDAY

SHORT-TERM PRIORITIES	SHORT-TERM ANTI-PRIORITIES

BUY YOURSELF TIME TO DECIDE

It is essential to take away the impulsivity element from our decision-making. If we don't make decisions in the heat of the moment, we are more likely to make a decision that aligns with our goals, and we won't regret it afterward. One way to achieve this is through understanding that we don't always need to immediately say "yes" to things. Of course, there are going to be situations where we might need to answer quickly, but we can still avoid choosing too fast by using an **enthusiastic, non-committal approach**.

Let me give you an example: A friend of yours calls you and says, *"We should really go with the girls for a two-day trip by the sea."* The idea sounds exciting and funny, but you don't want to commit to going yet. Instead of deciding, you could reply by saying, *"Wow, that sounds great! I'm not 100% sure I will be able to do it, but I can let you know soon!"*

Notice that you didn't say "yes." You expressed enthusiasm for something that you liked in the heat of the moment, but you didn't commit just yet one way or the other.

Also, if you keep the conversation going along those lines, you can ask questions to get more information and understand the details better. You can then close the conversation using something like "Let me check my schedule" or "I need to run this by my team," depending on the context of the request.

There are cases when, unfortunately, we are forced to reply quickly. But, even in those cases, there is one trick that I like to use to buy some extra time and cool down my brain. that I like to use.

Ask yourself, "Would I do this tomorrow?" The theory is that if you say yes, you either have free time to do it, or it is so crucial that you would cancel previous commitments to have enough time to focus on it. In addition, this is a way to stop passing on your problems to "future you," since you will have to deal with these things eventually.

SAY "NO" WHEN YOU SHOULD SAY "NO"

Okay, this is a terrible tip. If you could do this, you would not be reading this chapter. But let me elaborate. Sometimes it is good to remember that we are not the only ones who can do something. There are cases when you should feel free to say "no," knowing that you can delegate others to take on the task. This is especially true in a work environment. If you are with a team, the workload can be shared, and you should not jump on tasks in the heat of the moment if you don't feel like you can complete them.

"No" is not always negative. You can say "no" and still be supportive; there are things that you might not feel confident doing now, but things might change in the future.

Imagine you were invited for a weekend trip but took a previous commitment. You could say, *"This sounds cool, but unfortunately, I'm unavailable that weekend."* This is a positive "no"; you are sharing your support while explaining that you won't be able to attend.

At that point, three things might happen:

1. Your friends might go without you.
2. Your friends will try to reschedule for a better time that works for everyone. This might be good if the new option fits better in your schedule.
3. Your friends might try to pressure you into joining them.

Option three might sound scary, but it is easy to deal with if you stick to your initial commitment. Just repeat, "I'm sorry, but I'm not available that weekend" without over-explaining. If you don't over-explain, they can't disagree with your explanation. You might decide to add a few details, but you shouldn't feel stressed about it. Remember, you are just sticking to a previous commitment.

Also, avoid consolation commitments: *"I'm not available that weekend, but next time we should go to Paris together."* This is just committing to something you don't know if you will ever be able to do. Furthermore, it is likely to create problems in the future. Just stick to your original intention; you can be emphatic and supportive without committing to something you cannot do.

If they are used to us always saying "yes," people might get upset in the beginning. That's okay; you are not doing anything wrong. It is just a matter of helping them understand where your boundaries are and what you feel comfortable doing and not doing.

Let's practice how you would buy time or say "no" in hypothetical scenarios.

SCENARIO 1-A) A FRIEND OF YOURS TELLS YOU, "I WANT TO BOOK WITH THE GIRLS TO SPEND SOME TIME TOGETHER AT THE SPA THIS SUNDAY. ARE YOU COMING?"

YOU ALREADY HAVE BRUNCH ON SUNDAY MORNING, AND IT IS UNLIKELY YOU WILL BE ABLE TO DO BOTH. SO HOW WOULD YOU REFUSE THE INVITE?

_____

_____

_____

_____

_____

SCENARIO 1-B) A FRIEND OF YOURS TELLS YOU, "I WANT TO BOOK WITH THE GIRLS TO SPEND SOME TIME TOGETHER AT THE SPA THIS SUNDAY. ARE YOU COMING?"

YOU MIGHT BE ABLE TO DO IT, BUT YOU HAVE SCHEDULED A YOGA LESSON IN THE EARLY MORNING. TRY TO USE A NON-COMMITTAL APPROACH WHILE GATHERING MORE INFORMATION TO SEE IF YOU CAN MAKE IT.

_____

_____

_____

_____

SCENARIO 2) YOU ARE ATTENDING A COLLEGE CLASS, AND YOUR PROFESSOR SAYS SHE IS LOOKING FOR VOLUNTEERS TO WORK ON AN EXTRACURRICULAR PROJECT. YOUR FRIENDS SEEM INTERESTED, AND THEY ARE GOING TO VOLUNTEER. THEY SUGGEST THAT YOU SHOULD DO THE SAME, BUT YOU KNOW IT WOULD BE A BAD IDEA SINCE YOU CAN BARELY KEEP UP WITH YOUR STUDY WORKLOAD. THIS IS ONE OF THE CASES WHERE YOU SHOULD PROBABLY SAY NO WHILE SUPPORTING YOUR FRIENDS. HOW WOULD YOU DO IT?

SCENARIO 3) YOU HAVE A PRESTIGIOUS POSITION IN A DIGITAL COMPANY, AND YOU ARE MEETING WITH ONE OF THE MOST IMPORTANT STAKEHOLDERS. HE WANTS YOUR DEPARTMENT TO AGREE TO DO A PROJECT FOR HIM, AND HE WANTS YOU TO DELIVER IT VERY FAST. THEREFORE, HE ASKS YOU THE FOLLOWING QUESTION: "THE DETAILS WILL BE FINALIZED THIS WEEK, AND I WILL SEND ALL THE DOCUMENTATION BY FRIDAY. I WOULD LIKE THE PROJECT TO BE DELIVERED WITHIN TWO WEEKS MAXIMUM. CAN YOU DO IT?"

YOU ARE UNSURE IF YOUR DEPARTMENT CAN SATISFY HIS REQUESTS, AND YOU WANT TO BUY TIME WITHOUT MAKING ANY COMMITMENTS. HOW WOULD YOU DO IT?

SCENARIO 4) YOU WORK IN A RESTAURANT, AND YOUR COLLEAGUE ASKS IF YOU CAN TAKE HER SHIFT SINCE SHE WON'T BE ABLE TO WORK NEXT SATURDAY AT LUNCHTIME. YOU PLANNED TO USE YOUR SATURDAY MORNING TO DO YOGA AND WORK ON SOME PERSONAL PROJECTS. THIS IS ONE OF THE TIMES YOU WANT TO PROTECT YOUR COMMITMENTS AND SAY "NO." HOW WOULD YOU DO IT?

YOUR COLLEAGUE SEEMS UNHAPPY WITH YOUR RESPONSE; SHE IS PROBABLY USED TO YOU BEING MORE ACCOMMODATING. THAT'S AN EXCELLENT OPPORTUNITY TO PRACTICE ASSERTIVENESS WHILE NOT JUSTIFYING YOURSELF TOO MUCH. HOW WOULD YOU RE-ITERATE YOUR DECISION?

As you have seen during this chapter, saying "no" is necessary for our survival. We must filter the opportunities we want to seize from the pool of ideas and proposals that inevitably lead us to mess up our schedules and end up with nothing done. A workbook chapter that aims to cover as many problems as possible that we may encounter with ADHD has only a certain number of pages available.

Unfortunately, this topic alone would require a separate book, but I have good advice for you if you are interested.

If you found this topic interesting, consider Guard Your Yes—The Guidebook by Rene Brooks.

In a few hundred pages, you will learn everything there is to know about the art of saying "no" and protecting your plans!

In case you want to print the above exercises, you can find them in the online resources on pages 25 and 26.

CHAPTER 7

WORKING AND LEARNING FROM HOME

*T*he 2020 pandemic dramatically altered life around the globe, and one of its most prominent effects was forcing many people to take their work or studies from office buildings to living rooms.

Though the pandemic brought us many difficulties, it has also created some positive outcomes. Businesses have been pushed to embrace technology in new ways, and universities now offer online courses as a regular part of their curricula. This evolution promises exciting changes in how we work, study, and go about our day-to-day lives.

In many sectors, the worlds of work and learning are embracing a hybrid model based on remote and face-to-face activities. However, this new hybrid model also brings challenges for those like us who have ADHD, and for this reason, I decided to add a dedicated chapter.

This chapter may not apply to many professions, but it could shed new light on how to improve productivity for those that can be pursued from the comfort of home.

Speaking with my clients, I realized that the number of people who work or study from home at least a couple of days a week is on the rise. So, I hope this chapter will be helpful for a good chunk of readers.

Working or studying from home can provide tremendous opportunities for women with ADHD, allowing them to work in an environment that is better tailored to their needs. In addition, the flexible schedule and reduced distractions may enable these individuals to reach their maximum productivity potential.

The problem is that we are not in an ideal world where our ADHD brain behaves as we would like. Being able to build our schedule in some cases means that we would keep getting distracted all day long and not make any progress on our tasks. Also, a few distractions are good if you focus on the right thing. One day I spent four hours playing chess online just because I went into hyperfocus mode; I didn't do anything else. It wasn't my finest day.

Personally, I love working from home, but it is not so simple. For example, in the office and schools, there is an "infrastructure" that we don't see; these environments are set up to support productivity. Performing the same tasks at home might become challenging without this invisible infrastructure.

Luckily, the time of being forced to stay home is gone, and now, in most cases, it is up to the individual to decide whether to work or study from home. So, unlike in pandemic times, we don't have to adapt, and we can make our own choices.

Depending on your perspective, working and studying from home can be a blessing or a curse. In this chapter, we'll explore the upsides and downsides of remote work and some helpful tips I've picked up over the years.

STRUCTURE

Everyone has their morning rituals. If we have to go to school or work, we have the alarm clock set at a specific time. We know when to shower, have breakfast, get dressed, and leave the house.

Both at school and in the office, there is a clear timetable. For example, we have class schedules and classrooms; we know when a lesson starts and ends. At work, there are meetings; it is clear when it is time to work and when it is time to brainstorm.

While working or studying from home, this rigid schedule may disappear. Although it is tempting to go from bed to desk, not having your morning ritual is dangerous.

One of the many challenges that ADHD brains encounter is difficulty keeping track of the time that passes. This problem has been studied from multiple angles, and various experts agree on the relationship between ADHD and time blindness:

> "*Practical approaches to time perception and its evaluation have shown that individuals with ADHD have difficulties in time estimation and discrimination activities as well as having the feeling that time is passing by without them being able to complete tasks accurately and well.*" (Ptacek, et al., 2019)

An excellent way to deal with time blindness is to use a strategy discussed in the time management section. We can resort to **time blocking**. This strategy consists of blocking time slots during the day for specific activities. We are practically creating a schedule that will represent the structure of our day.

Also, remember that, thanks to our ADHD brain, we tend to underestimate how long it takes to perform a particular activity. Therefore, I highly recommend you overestimate the blocks in your schedule to have enough time to complete and transition from one task to another.

As a bonus, you will feel accomplished when you finish doing something sooner than expected!

TRANSITIONS AND RITUALS

You could also consider including transition-time slots in your schedule to make it more transparent that you should move from one activity to another. The process of moving from one task to another is called set-shifting, and it is one of the functions that ADHD might impair.

For example, think about when you go to work or school. The journey represents your transition time. If, when you leave home, you do not feel ready to start working or studying, by the time you arrive, your mind will have almost certainly made the transition, and you will feel prepared.

Without travel, you would find yourself straight to school or work, but you may not be ready to perform immediately. Transition time is essential to decompress and prepare for what we have in front of us. Our brain needs time between tasks, and this is a need that should not be ignored.

If we have implicit transition times in our schedule when we go to work or school, we should make it explicit when we work or learn at home.

One way to help us transition from one thing to another is to create rituals. For example, my ritual for transitioning out of work is to take a nice walk with my dog. It allows me to relax and leave the stress of the day behind. Another ritual I have in the morning to wake up and start the day is to meditate for 10 minutes.

Moreover, before starting work after the lunch break, I watch a 10-minute video on YouTube. I try to choose something that is not frivolous, perhaps a technical video or scientific curiosity, to create the right mood for returning to work.

Rituals are helpful; they are the pillars on which we can build our day, and we can always count on them to help us move efficiently from one commitment to another on our calendar.

Now it's your turn. Try to think of rituals to help you better mark your day and support your transitions. Remember, the purpose of a ritual is to create a routine; it is crucial that you choose something you like and won't mind doing.

RITUAL 1:

RITUAL 2:

RITUAL 3:

ACCOUNTABILITY

When we are in school, the teacher checks that we do the exercises. At work, the boss checks that we carry out the assigned tasks. This control mechanism is also a reward system; we are often proud to show our professors or boss the work that we've done.

At home, we are alone. Nobody controls us in the same way, and there are countless ways to do other things while we pretend to work. One way to stem this problem is to resort to an accountability system.

Accountability is a recurring topic regarding people with ADHD. If you have read online texts, watched videos on YouTube, or followed courses of any kind, at some point, accountability will be mentioned.

The fact that it is proposed as a solution to many problems caused by ADHD is both annoying and reassuring. Trusting other people and finding someone to monitor our progress is bothersome and sometimes challenging. We all realize sooner or later that there are no easy solutions to our problems, but at the same time, with one (potentially annoying) single solution, we can deal with multiple ADHD problems.

When we work or study from home, relying on an **accountability buddy** is one of the best ways to ensure things get done.

SOCIALIZE

Both at work and at school, we have a lot of social interactions. We spend time with colleagues and friends over lunch, on breaks, and at many other occasions.

In these environments, we sometimes have too many social interactions, especially if we fall into the category of introverts.

The problem is that, at home, we have much fewer social interactions, and even for an introverted person, it is essential to spend some time with other people.

It is important when we work or study from home to find ways to socialize and allocate enough time to do so during our day.

With many social situations now becoming increasingly digital, I discovered there are still many ways to make meaningful connections. So, here's some helpful advice on how you can stay connected:

- Create a coffee break in your calendar where you have a call with your friends or people on your team. The purpose is not to discuss work but to hang out as you would during a break.

- Download the Netflix party extension for the Google Chrome browser so you can organize breaks where you watch an episode of a TV series you love together.

- Organize calls with people instead of exchanging just a few chat messages.

- If you work in a team, arrange regular calls during the week.

- Go for a walk during your lunch break; you might buy yourself a sandwich or a salad at the shop next door. It's an excellent excuse to have some minimal social interaction.

- Organize virtual lunches or happy hours with colleagues and friends so as not to eat alone.

CUES

We have various cues associated with starting our work or studies. For example, when a teacher starts talking, that is the signal that we need to start paying attention and that the lesson has begun.

If we are in the library, we isolate ourselves with headphones and listen to music with books in front of us, and that is the signal that it is time to study.

When we are at home, most of the cues we receive prompt us to do other things. As a result, our homes are sources of constant distraction. For example, we can get signals that suggest we clean, play, or do other stuff while we are supposed to work or study.

To avoid being bombarded with distractions, we want to create clear cues that it is time to start studying or working. But, of course, the best cues are the ones we are already familiar with. For example,

When I put my headphones on and sit at the desk, it's time to work.

Infinite cues can be created. Here are some ideas to build a mental separation between work/study and free time:

- Have a dedicated workspace that doesn't feel the same as the rest of the house.

- Have a mouse and keyboard dedicated only to work/study.

- Wear different clothes when you work or study. It is not necessary to dress like you would in the office, but a more elegant blouse can help our brains to understand that we are in work/study mode.

Also, use cues for other people living with you if you don't want to be interrupted. You can place a sign on your desk or home office door using various colors. Based on the color displayed, those who live with you will know if it is okay to interrupt you. Also, share your calendar with them so they know when you're free.

These are just ideas. It makes no sense to apply them all together. Their usefulness will vary from person to person, and I suggest my clients create their cues only when they realize they need them.

In the next exercise, think of four work/home study situations in which you feel you need cues to perform better. Next, try to define your cues for those situations.

SITUATION 1:

_____

_____

CUE THAT I WILL USE:

_____

_____

_____

_____

_____

SITUATION 2:

_____

_____

CUE THAT I WILL USE:

_____

_____

_____

_____

_____

SITUATION 3:

_____

_____

CUE THAT I WILL USE:

_____

_____

_____

_____

_____

SITUATION 4:

_____

_____

CUE THAT I WILL USE:

_____

_____

_____

_____

_____

Before closing this section, I would like to give you some advice. Be kinder to yourself when you work or study from home. Performing in a different environment takes work and requires an adaptation phase. Also, doing the work is essential, but even more important is being happy with yourself.

Working or studying from home can be a difficult balance to strike, but don't let yourself feel guilty if you don't accomplish all your goals right away. Instead, take the time to appreciate how this new lifestyle may have improved other aspects of your life.

CHAPTER 8
DECLUTTER YOUR LIFE

*F*rom the previous chapters, you will have understood by now that women living with ADHD tend to have problems with executive functions.

In this section, we will focus on one of them; namely, "inhibition":

> *"Inhibitory control (one of the core executive functions) involves being able to control one's attention, behavior, thoughts, and/or emotions to override a strong internal predisposition or external lure, and instead do what's more appropriate or needed."*
> (A., 2013)

Our brain's lack of working inhibitory control often leads us to take on too much.

While we work on one thing, we realize that we should also take care of other things. Unfortunately, this leads us to multitask on many items and generally not finish any of them.

This problem, if observed from the house management point of view, frequently leads to chaos and difficulty in organizing our home environment.

HOUSE DECLUTTERING

One way to help ourselves with inhibition is the "**body double technique**." A person in the room can be a gentle reminder of what we should do and help us keep the focus on what is important.

Sometimes, however, the problems must be taken more head-on, and it is for these cases that there are slightly more invasive and effective techniques. As usual, we will tackle the problem in small steps and use our best ally, the list!

I know what you're thinking; *"Another list system? I'm tired of making lists of everything in my life."* You're right; it's annoying and unfair that we must work hard to carry out seemingly simple operations. But, unfortunately, our brain works differently from neurotypical people, bringing us advantages and disadvantages.

Give this system a chance. It's annoying, but if you try, you might be pleasantly surprised by the results.

Let's start by breaking down the problem of cleaning and organizing our home one room at a time. First, we want to create a list of tasks for each room. The idea is to break down the thought of "This is a mess, I don't know where to start from" into a much smaller set of problems.

The initial goal is to understand how much there is to do, which room will require a few minutes of work, and which will require hours.

The good news is that once you've filled out your list, you're unlikely to need to do it again soon. This is because the tasks to do in each room rarely change; every so often, there will be something more or less to do, but you can think of this list as your blueprint to reuse as long as you live in the same house. You can make many copies of it to use whenever necessary.

So, let's start by filling in the following pages with your tasks as shown in the example.

As always, you can download more of these sheets from the online resources. In particular, you'll find these on page 31.

ROOM NAME: Kitchen

TASKS LIST:

- ☑ Do the dishes
- ☑ Clean countertops and surfaces
- ☑ Clean the floor
- ☐ Check the fridge for expired food
- ☐ (Optional) clean the fridge
- ☐

ROOM NAME:

TASKS LIST:

- ☐
- ☐
- ☐
- ☐
- ☐
- ☐

ROOM NAME: _____

TASKS LIST:

- ☐ _____
- ☐ _____
- ☐ _____
- ☐ _____
- ☐ _____
- ☐ _____

ROOM NAME: _____

TASKS LIST:

- ☐ _____
- ☐ _____
- ☐ _____
- ☐ _____
- ☐ _____
- ☐ _____

ROOM NAME: _____

TASKS LIST:

- ☐ _____
- ☐ _____
- ☐ _____
- ☐ _____
- ☐ _____
- ☐ _____

ROOM NAME: _____

TASKS LIST:

- ☐ _____
- ☐ _____
- ☐ _____
- ☐ _____
- ☐ _____
- ☐ _____

ROOM NAME: _____

TASKS LIST:

☐ _____

☐ _____

☐ _____

☐ _____

☐ _____

☐ _____

ROOM NAME: _____

TASKS LIST:

☐ _____

☐ _____

☐ _____

☐ _____

☐ _____

☐ _____

Now that we have our battle plan, let's break down the complicated task of fixing up our house and focus on tackling it piece by piece. We can move closer to a tidier home with each little step forward. We will start with the room we think is most straightforward.

Despite our battle plan, there is still the risk that our brains will get distracted by other things or decide to focus too much on one part of a single task. Therefore, an effective strategy to not dwell on a single thing indefinitely is to **remove the distraction from our sight**.

Imagine that we are dealing with a pair of our shoes. We don't know what to do with them; should we throw them away? Keep them? Where do we put them?

If you need more than a minute to decide, maybe it's time to remove the distraction and postpone the issue. Take your shoes and put them somewhere else, away from the room you're tidying up. Now, go back immediately without looking back.

You will only face the "shoe problem" when you finish the scheduled tasks.

Also, remember to tick off tasks on your list as they are completed. It will be an energy boost whenever you can finally remove an item from the list.

I've used this system several times, and it works, but I must confess, I've never been able to do all the tasks on my list at once. The problem is that even if you have a solid system, you must apply it with the proper mental discipline.

In some cases, I get distracted too easily. However, I'm still grateful for the progress this system has allowed me to make. Instead of striving for the elusive, unattainable standard of perfection, we should appreciate and accept what is "normal."

Let's say my house isn't as chaotic as before, but at the same time, it doesn't look like something out of a magazine, which is good enough!

DEAL WITH THE PAPER MONSTER

Okay, now we have a system to tidy up the house, but what can we do about the **paper monster**?

If you're anything like me, you'll have tons of paper around. Notes, bills, documents, lists, to-dos, calendars, reminders, and everything that arrives in the mailbox that we keep thinking we will check later but we never do.

To avoid seeing our house invaded by paper, we must do something. We can break down the paper monster by adopting a simple **pile system**.

The first thing we want to do is divide our paper monster into different piles:

ACTION PILE   FILE PILE   SLOW PAPER PILE

RECYCLING PILE   TRASH PILE

Action pile: This pile contains any letter, document, or simple piece of paper that will lead us to do something. Examples of what we might find in this pile are bills to pay or something to read more carefully.

File pile: This pile contains letters and documents we must keep in our personal archives. Examples of what we might find in this pile are house documents, paid bills, important communications, etc.

Recycling pile: This pile contains all documents intended for recycling. Remember that it is essential not to throw away entire documents that contain your personal data. Examples of sensitive data are your social security number, bank account numbers, etc. You can tear the papers if you don't have a shredder. Unfortunately, shredded documents are unsuitable for recycling, as the fibers are not long enough. So, we'll throw them in the trash.

Trash pile: This pile contains everything we want to throw away, but unfortunately, it can't be recycled.

Slow paper pile: This stack probably contains junk documents, but we're not 100% sure, and we want to check them carefully. We only want to ensure that it doesn't contain important documents associated with deadlines, such as utility bills. We will revisit this stack later.

If you are not sure what you should keep on file and what you should throw away, here are some simple rules that might help you:

Documents to keep for seven years or longer: tax records, tax returns and related documents, home remodeling projects, buying or selling assets, W-2 forms, 1099 forms

Documents to keep for at least one year: bank and credit card statements, investment statements, receipts for large purchases, paid medical bills (hold them longer if part of unresolved insurance dispute)

Also, remember that most of these documents are available online now, so it is simple to download them again if necessary.

Once we've split all the paper into piles, it's time to move on to the next step. As for the garbage and recycling pile, there's not much else to do. So let's throw the paper in the bins, and we can go and concentrate on the other piles.

We'll focus on the slow paper pile only later, so let's take all the documents in this pile, put them in a box, and leave it alone for now.

Probably more than half of the paper monster is gone by now.

Let us now deal with the file pile. First, we will need labels and colored folders. I use a color scheme to divide documents by topic:

Red: school-related/work-related documents

Blue: house-related documents

Green: money-related documents

Usually, what I do is archive the documents by month. Take, for example, financial documents (green folders).

Every year, I archive 12 green folders. I label each one with the month and year and add all the related documents. It's simple, easy, and leaves no room for doubt.

Optionally, you can create subfolders in each folder and label them separately in case you have a large volume of documents. In my case, it's not necessary; indeed, in some cases, I'm merging a few months if I don't have enough documents to justify wasting a folder.

You can follow this system or build the filing system you prefer; the important thing is to be consistent.

Next is the action pile. This is perhaps the slowest and most tedious part. We have to go document by document and understand what actions are needed. Multiple sessions may be required to complete the task depending on the size of your action pile.

I usually do the first scan by scrolling through the documents, and then I write the actions I need to take on them in pencil.

I don't want to limit myself to generic activities such as "pay the bill." Instead, I want to list specific duties, such as "Call this phone number," "Make an appointment with the bank for next week," or "Make a deposit to this account."

Once you understand the actions associated with each document, I suggest you move the documents to places where it is easier for you to perform them. For example, leave the document near your computer if you need to go to the bank's website to check something. If you need to make an appointment by telephone, leave the document with the relevant action near the phone.

When the task on the document is completed, you can move it to your archive or throw it away, depending on what is best.

Lastly, there is the slow paper pile. As already mentioned, this stack contains no critical documents. We can then take our time and decide if there is anything inside that makes sense to archive or move all the contents to the recycling and trash piles.

Now that we've disposed of all the piles, we've finally defeated the paper monster. However, to prevent it from reappearing, it is important to apply this system regularly. Usually, the first time is the most difficult, given the number of documents that are typically accumulated, but the subsequent times should be easier.

CHAPTER 9

ADHD-PROOF YOUR FINANCES

*M*anaging money for women with ADHD is quite complex. Procrastination, disorganization, and impulsivity determine how well we manage our money.

> *"Daily routines in Western societies require people to pay bills on time, make rent and mortgage payments, and keep track of investments and savings. Yet, despite awareness that adults with ADHD face difficulties managing these and other financials, the extent of such difficulties and their associations with individual well-being have not been evaluated with objective data. According to self-reports, adults with ADHD are more financially dependent on family members, face more difficulties paying bills, open fewer savings accounts, use credit cards more compulsively, and are more likely to use very high interest rate borrowing, such as pawnshops and payday loans, than others in the population."* (Beauchaine T. P., 2020)

Fortunately, various techniques can come to our rescue. In this chapter, I'll share the best strategies and my learnings to make things more manageable.

IMPROVE YOUR CREDIT SCORE

The credit score is nothing more than a numerical index used in many countries of the world to determine how reliable a person is from a monetary point of view. Banks and lenders use this score to decide whether to grant us a loan or mortgage or entrust us with money.

Lenders want to know if we can repay the debt, so they assess our income and determine whether we are reliable and will repay it. The credit score is a way to measure each person from this point of view.

Our ADHD brain may prevent us from having a good credit score. This happens because of various factors:

- **Impulsivity** leads us from time to time to buy things that we may not be able to afford.

- **Procrastination** leads us to miss deadlines and not pay bills on time.

- **Poor planning** leads us to create expenses that we will hardly be able to repay in the long run.

These aspects vary in severity from person to person. For example, some individuals have ADHD and can manage their finances reasonably well, while others easily fall into the traps created by their brains.

The final result, however, does not change; all of us, more or less, pay the ADHD tax. Fines, fees, and higher interest rates affect ADHD people much more frequently than neurotypical people.

One of the most annoying things is how easy it is to mess up our credit scores. Building a good credit score takes years, but a few unpaid expenses are enough to see it drop inexorably.

Okay, but what can we do if our credit score is already low? How can we improve it quickly and keep it at an acceptable level?

An immediate solution does not exist, but there are various things we can do to increase our credit score in a reasonably short time.

- **Dispute problems on credit reports.** This is not particularly hard to do and typically involves reaching out to your credit reporting company and explaining in writing what is wrong. The act of disputing items on your credit report does not hurt your score, but remember that cardholders can face the consequences of false claims.

- **Get added as an authorized user on someone else's card with a good credit history.** This will not significantly impact your credit score, as you are not responsible for paying the bill, but it's an easy and risk-free way to increase your credit score by a few points.

- **Pay down credit card balances if you have the money to do it.** Taking your debt exposure to zero by paying off your credit cards is one of the best ways to boost your credit score. Obviously, this is easier said than done; not everyone has the financial means to repay their debt in full.

- **Avoid making multiple applications if you are trying to get a loan or a mortgage.** If a bank has rejected your request, wait at least 30 days before trying with a different bank. Multiple requests in a short period could further lower your credit score.

- **Try Experian Boost.** Experian is an American–Irish multinational data analytics and consumer credit reporting company that allows you to add a broader range of charges to your credit score calculation. For example, automated expenses such as household bills, streaming services, etc., can be added. Since these expenses are automated, we will hardly miss payments, and our credit score will benefit.

- **Consider getting a credit-building card.** This type of card allows you to build your credit score quickly. They are not difficult to obtain and are characterized by a low spending limit and a high interest rate. I would not suggest getting this card to anyone as it introduces a high risk factor. Missing a payment with this card can become quite expensive due to the interest charged. If you decide to take a credit-building card, make sure that the spending limit associated with it is low enough not to allow you any crazy spending and immediately activate the automatic monthly payments in full of the debt.

The problem, however, is not how to raise our credit score but how to maintain it. Unfortunately, for women who have ADHD, going in and out of small or big financial crises is quite common, and none of the above tips give us peace of mind in the long run.

Paraphrasing Rick Webster, founder and CEO of Rena-Fi, a financial literacy education company dedicated to creating ADHD-friendly resources and support systems:

> *"When we are in a crisis, in many ways it is too late. We have fewer choices available, and the deeper into the crisis we get, the fewer options we have. We can not afford certain expenses, or we are just late paying them. So we put our heads in the sand and don't take any action. At this point, we are also in the throes of an emotional pre-meltdown, making it very difficult to make good decisions. So we solve the problems with little thought about the long-term impact and set ourselves up for the next crisis. This is all part of the ADHD tax that we pay, and we must find a way to be more proactive in our lives."*

Fortunately, there are people in the world who specialize in ADHD money management who have developed various strategies tested over the years to minimize the risk of falling back into the problem of a low credit score.

USE AUTOMATION

While it is recommended that neurotypical people keep track of cash with computerized systems and applications, for people with ADHD, the opposite is true. To set up complicated systems, we must also want to use them constantly. However, due to the way our brain works, it is very likely that once these systems are set up, we will simply forget to use them.

What we want to do instead is automate as much as possible to have fewer things to keep in mind. We have to play on our strengths and not let our weaknesses bring us down, and remembering to do something is not our strong suit.

Okay, but what can we do on a practical level? Here are some ideas to reduce the number of things you have to think about:

- **Set up two checking accounts**—one for day-to-day spending and one for bill paying. Get your salary automatically paid in the "day-to-day spending" account. Set an auto-transfer on payday from the "day-to-day spending" account into the "bills account." Set auto pay from the "bills account" to ensure that bills get auto-drawn. In this way, your bills will always be paid automatically, and you will always have funds in your account available to pay them.

- Through internet banking or contacting your bank directly, **set up automatic alert messages** to notify you when your accounts go below a certain funds threshold, or you are exceeding your expenses budget. This way, you can avoid overdraft fees.

- If there are regular payments that you can't automate, **set up alerts to remind you that it's time to make these payments**. Add the deadline to your schedule and be sure they don't go unnoticed!

- **Create a savings account and set up an automatic transfer on payday** to move the amount you want into the savings account each month. Something can always go wrong; automatically setting aside some money can be an essential buffer for future contingencies. The basic idea is that you can't spend money that isn't in your account, and transferring it into your savings account immediately after you receive your paycheck is the best way to protect your money.

- **Sign up for a credit tracking app like Experian or Credit Karma** to be automatically notified if anything changes in your credit score.

BUILD A SAFETY NET

Spending all the money we earn every month would be like constantly living on the edge, and any unexpected expense would push us beyond our budget.

We want to avoid creating debt that we may have difficulty repaying, which could negatively impact our credit score. Unfortunately, some people have no alternatives, but we can build a safety net in most cases.

The idea is to intentionally spend less than we earn and save a certain amount for emergencies. However, unlike a savings account, this money must always be available, so we can't afford to block it for long periods to have a higher interest rate. This fund is there for the next time our brain decides to go full ADHD, and instead of building up debt, we can use our safety net to repay the damage.

Building a safety net should be your priority over paying off any debt quickly. Unlike a neurotypical person, paying off debt immediately is only a short-term solution for us. With ADHD, the chances of missing a payment or making an impulse buy are common occurrences, and without a safety net, falling back into debt is almost guaranteed.

Also, keep in mind that there are various strategies to pay your debt efficiently. One of the most effective is the **"Snowball" method**.

This straightforward strategy applies perfectly to people with multiple debts accumulated over time. We first want to list all the debts and sort them from smallest to largest, ignoring the associated interest rates. At this point, we want to make the minimum payment for every debt except the smallest. We will try to pay the smallest debt as much as possible to pay it off quickly. Please remember that the safety net takes priority, so you should regularly pay in your safety net before dealing with your debts. We want to repeat the process until the smallest debt is paid off and then move on to the next.

Usually, when I explain this strategy, the first thing that is said to me is that I have not considered interest rates. The idea is simple. Whatever the interest rate on your most significant debts, it will take a long time for your payments to start having a real effect by reducing the interest you pay.

By paying off minor debts immediately, however, you can gradually concentrate your efforts on a small number of debts.

This will create a snowball effect where, initially, you will only see a few small debts being paid off. However, when the number of minimum payments gets smaller, you will start to pay off your debts faster. Also, seeing the number of debts reduced is a source of motivation, and having fewer things to think about can help reduce stress.

PREVENT IMPULSE SPENDING

Impulse spending is an issue for many people with ADHD and can completely derail our financial well-being. The tendency to spend on impulse is something challenging to eradicate, and it is entirely unrealistic to expect to be able to manage it perfectly.

According to Nerd Wallet: "Almost half of Americans say that emotions cause them to spend more than they can reasonably afford. With stress, excitement, and sadness being the top emotions associated with overspending."

If we apply the same statistic to people with ADHD, we will see that this number is much higher. We must understand that managing our finances is not controlling our bank accounts. We must address our emotions and sometimes find the time to stop and check in with ourselves to make sure that we are actually doing the right thing.

Managing our emotions is not easy, but we can create a system that limits our impulsive spending and, therefore, the potential damage we can do to our finances. I suggest using a budgeting system that prevents us from spending more than a certain amount each month.

Creating this system is simple. First, we create a new bank account in which we will automatically deposit a certain amount every month. This sum will represent **our budget for impulse spending**. If the account is empty, we can't do any more impulse shopping this month.

We then configure Amazon and other online shops we frequently use so that they use a card directly linked to this account by default. This way, when we buy our next item on Amazon, the purchase will be rejected without funds in the account. Obviously, we could decide to change the payment method at the purchase time, but seeing the transaction initially declined and the overhead required to change the payment method should be enough to make us slow down and reflect on whether we need this new item.

Another important tip for reducing impulse buying is to **ensure your basic needs are met before shopping**. You also want to **ensure you are not in a fragile or extreme emotional state**. Basically, avoid grocery shopping if you're hungry, or don't go shopping for clothing if you're sad, angry, or frustrated. If we take these factors out of the equation, we are much more likely to be able to control our impulse to buy things.

There are also other tricks you can try to adopt when you are about to buy an item. One of them is to **use a checklist before completing the purchase**.

Before you pay, ask yourself the following questions:

- Do I need this?/Do they need this? (in case you are buying a gift)
- How do I feel?
- What happens if I buy it later?
- How will I pay for it?
- Where will I put it?

If, after answering these questions, you still intend to make the purchase, it probably isn't an impulse spend.

If you shop online, **I suggest you leave the item you want in your cart or wishlist for at least 24 hours**. This should give you enough time to ponder whether it's an item you need.

The advice for important purchases is always to first **chat with your partner or friends**. In general, what you want to do is slow down enough for the impulse to disappear so that you can make an objective decision.

By following these tips and creating a dedicated budget, you can worry much less about impulse purchases. Of course, we can't expect to be perfect, and no one can ask us that, but we can create an infrastructure that minimizes the possibility of making choices we may regret in the future. Also, remember that doing a little shopping is therapeutic, and from time to time, buying something we want is a way to take care of ourselves.

CHAPTER 10
ADHD AND SOCIAL SKILLS

*H*ave you ever felt that sometimes everyone knows how to play the social game aside from you? If that's the case, trust me, you are not alone!

> *"ADHD is frequently associated with impaired social functioning. These social behavioral difficulties begin in childhood for children with ADHD, and continue through adolescence and into adulthood"* (Aduen P. A., 2018)

It is not uncommon for women with ADHD to watch social interactions as outsiders, mainly trying to figure out what to do. But, as usual, what seems incredibly easy for others is complicated and alien to us.

Neurotypical people have learned these social skills without difficulty at an early age, and this has formed a solid foundation on which they have developed their interactions over the years. Learning these skills occurs mainly through observation at an early age. Children play at imitating grownups, copy the behavior of their friends, and get implicit feedback that helps them refine their social abilities.

Children with ADHD often don't have all the tools to refine their skills equally and would need a different learning path to achieve the same results. Unfortunately, social acceptance is either a downward spiral or an upward spiral. People with good social skills are rewarded with the acceptance of their peers, making it easier for them to improve their skills further.

People with ADHD who already have difficulty playing the social game are often met with social rejection, which limits opportunities to learn and improve. This is one of the main reasons our social skills are not as refined as those of our peers in adulthood.

Furthermore, this creates strong emotional baggage. I have no shame in saying that I rarely participated in group activities and had very few female friends as a child. This led me into a depression that lasted for a few years— not being accepted and struggling to understand why is one of the most terrible feelings. Unfortunately, this is a pervasive reality for women with ADHD.

Fortunately for us, since I was a child, many studies have shown the relationship between ADHD and social skills. In addition, various methods have proven effective for women suffering from this problem.

OWN UP TO YOUR TENDENCY TO INTERRUPT

Women with ADHD tend to be highly creative; their brains work a thousand miles per hour, creating new ideas all the time. The price to pay is having all these ideas in our heads that are just waiting to come out. Unfortunately, this can lead us to interrupt in conversations from time to time. Sometimes we can bring out some exciting ideas, but other times our interlocutor may be confused or unclear on whether we are actually listening.

When I was in primary school, the teacher asked me why I kept interrupting the lesson, and I remember my response was something like, *"I thought things, so I said them."*

This is a naive way to express our problem; sometimes, we have fewer filters between the brain and mouth.

Immediately saying what we think is also influenced by our emotions. If we are excited, anxious, or scared, we may be unable to control ourselves as we would like, amplifying the problem.

The best way to remedy the issue is to rely on others and be open. We must first remember that we are adults who are interacting with adults. Therefore, there is no shame in explaining our problem to the people we interact with, so they know what to expect.

Our brain works differently from neurotypical people. We work hard all our lives to cohabitate with our ADHD, and if the people we talk to can't handle some interruptions, maybe it's best not to deal with them. They probably don't care that much about us.

All my friends know about my problem. I do my best to control myself, and they accept me the way I am. Of course, it's not an ideal solution, but we love each other and make it work.

When I meet new people, and I know I will be in a stressful situation, the first thing I do is explain my problem openly.

Even when fresh out of college and looking for a job, I informed the interviewers that my ADHD would undoubtedly play a role during our conversation. I wanted them to know that my occasional interruptions were not meant as disrespect but as a sign of enthusiasm and interest in joining their team.

Once the problem was explained, especially in the business environment, I rarely found people who weren't accommodating and empathetic.

In less formal discussions, you can ask a dear friend for help. The idea is to use tactile feedback to stop you when you're overdoing it. You can decide on a signal, such as touching your arm or leg, as your secret communication method. Your friend will use this signal to tell you that you are losing control of the conversation; it is time to slow down, take a breath, and listen to the other people.

SHOW YOU ARE INTERESTED

It's easy to disengage when a conversation gets boring or our focus shifts to something else. However, at these times, we can use active listening skills to show interest in the conversation and that we genuinely care.

There are various ways to stay engaged and display curiosity:

- Ask follow-up questions, or you can periodically summarize the speaker's comments if it is a complex discussion.

- Try not to form counterarguments while the other person is still speaking.

- If you see your concentration drop, try to repeat in your mind what the other person is saying.

- Use your body language to show that you are engaged; nod, smile, and use facial expressions. Adopt an open and interested posture.

DON'T BE A CLOSE TALKER

When you are having a conversation, one of the most annoying things is having someone invade your personal space. No one likes to talk to someone within an inch of their face. If you've never had this happen, you could be the close talker. This behavior can happen for various reasons; the desire to be heard, insecurity, or the desire to convince the interlocutor that our opinion is valid. But that's not all; another critical reason is inherent in how our ADHD brain works.

In our brain, there are various areas; among these, we find the amygdala and the hippocampus. According to a 2006 study, these areas are related to ADHD symptoms and show a slightly altered morphology:

> "Limbic structures [amygdala and hippocampus] are implicated in the genesis of attention-deficit/hyperactivity disorder (ADHD) by the presence of mood and cognitive disturbances in affected individuals and by elevated rates of mood disorders in family members of probands with ADHD.

[...] The hippocampus was larger bilaterally in the ADHD group than in the control group. Detailed surface analyses of the hippocampus further localized these differences to an enlarged head of the hippocampus in the ADHD group.

[...] Disrupted connections between the amygdala and orbitofrontal cortex may contribute to behavioral disinhibition. Our findings suggest the involvement of the limbic system in the pathophysiology of ADHD." (Plessen K. J., 2006)

It was only in 2009, however, that scientists from the California Institute of Technology could prove the relationship between the amygdala and the sense of personal space without a shadow of a doubt.

"The amygdala plays key roles in emotion and social cognition, but how this translates to face-to-face interactions involving real people remains unknown. We found that an individual with complete amygdala lesions lacked any sense of personal space. Furthermore, healthy individuals showed amygdala activation upon close personal proximity. The amygdala may be required to trigger the strong emotional reactions normally following personal space violations, thus regulating interpersonal distance in humans." (Kennedy DP, 2009)

Our amygdala is very far from being damaged like the test subject, and not all people with ADHD have issues with personal space. Still, the correlation between the amygdala and respect for personal space exists.

This is why, **if you are a close talker, you may not realize it because your amygdala works slightly differently than that of a neurotypical person.**

Whatever the reason, respecting each other's personal space when conversing is essential. Even if our brain doesn't implicitly tell us to do it, we can take measures using active thinking. The best way to do this is to actively consider keeping a "safe distance" from the person we are talking to.

Okay, but if our ADHD brain doesn't tell us what the correct distance is, how can we find it?

I could tell you that the typical American will maintain a distance of roughly 1.5 to 3 feet from their conversation partner. Still, I doubt you want to walk around with a measuring tape.

The easiest thing to do is **observe how our interlocutor reacts**. I'm not talking about complex facial expressions but their entire body.

Start the conversation just over a step away from your conversation partner, and one of these things will happen:

- **Your partner stands still in their position**, which probably means that the distance for conversation is adequate.

- **Your partner takes a step forward**. This probably means the distance was too much, and your partner felt the need to reduce it. You don't need to do anything; your partner has done the work for you by finding the most appropriate distance to converse.

- **Your partner leans forward**. This is a sign that you are too distant, but your partner does not seem to take the initiative. Get just a little bit closer to find the optimal distance.

- **Your partner takes a step back**. This means that you have inadvertently invaded their personal space. The conversation distance is now correct; you don't have to do anything.

- **Your partner leans back**. This means that your partner is not comfortable. Take the initiative and back away slightly.

One thing you could do, especially if you have difficulty interpreting body language, is to get help from a friend or relative. For example, you can stage conversations where your friend uses their body language to help you find the most appropriate distance.

I know this may seem extremely simple to many but for some people with ADHD, having to actively think about where they physically stand during a conversation is a real problem.

I hope this method can help you!

SPOT THE SOCIAL CUES

Having ADHD can make it challenging to recognize the social cues people send when the interaction with them isn't going well. For example, this can happen when we speak too loudly, interrupt the speaker, invade their space, or in other circumstances.

Interpreting non-verbal communication is a very complex skill. Still, some signals can be interpreted by everyone and give us a clear idea of how the person we are conversing with is feeling.

- **Eye contact**: If someone is holding your gaze steady, this is usually a sign that the person is engaged in the conversation. On the other hand, if we see that the person we are talking to tends to avoid our gaze, this can signify that they are not involved in the conversation or feel uncomfortable. Keep in mind that looking a person in the eye is considered rude in some cultures; in this case, we will not be able to use this signal to interpret the mood of the conversation.

- **Looking down at their phones**: If you see a person who, during a conversation, is constantly distracted by looking at their mobile phone, this, in addition to being a lack of respect, shows a lack of involvement in the conversation. This applies to both sides. Sometimes, when we get a new notification on our phone, we want to immediately look at what it is, but it is better to try to resist and show the person we are conversing with that they are our priority.

- **Sighing or yawning**: This is an easy signal to interpret. Usually, someone who acts this way is not involved in the conversation, or else they are just exhausted.

- **Silence**: Most people are uncomfortable with those awkward pauses, making them a social cue that's easy to recognize. If with people we know, this can be a sign of minor importance; for people we are learning to know, this can indicate a conversation that is not going very well.

- **Facing toward or away**: If someone is facing us, this generally indicates a higher level of involvement. On the other hand, if a person seems to be pointing their body in another direction, this could signify that they are not feeling at ease and are looking for a way out of the conversation.

Countless other signals are part of a person's body language. For example, posture, proximity, facial expressions, how we smile, mirroring, tone of voice, physical touch, etc.

Unfortunately, not all of them are as easily readable as the ones listed above, but we can train ourselves to interpret the easier ones!

Let's start with some easy images, and we can work our way up.

Look at the woman in the image below.

How do you think she feels?

_____

_____

Do you notice any of the social cues mentioned in this chapter?

_____

_____

Look at the woman in the image below.

How do you think she feels?

_____

_____

_____

_____

Do you notice any of the social cues mentioned in this chapter?

_____

_____

_____

_____

Look at the man in the image below.

How do you think he feels?

_____

_____

_____

_____

Do you notice any of the social cues mentioned in this chapter?

_____

_____

_____

_____

The people in the above pictures are extreme examples, almost caricatured, but I can assure you that many of the social signals sent to us daily are nearly as clear as those shown in the images above.

For those who want to check their answers, here is the solution:

- **First image:** The woman feels ignored and little considered. We can see how the man uses his cell phone instead of engaging in conversation, and there is no eye contact between the two.

- **Second image:** The woman looks bored and uninterested. There is no eye contact between the two. The woman turned her head as if to look for a way out of the situation.

- **Third image:** The man does not seem interested; there is no eye contact between the two, and the body is oriented so as not to look at the woman.

One way to improve our ability to recognize these social cues is to train in the field by working on our observation skills. The idea is simple: If we remove ourselves from the equation, we can observe a social situation without the stress of participating in it.

Next time you're out, look at the strangers around you for a few seconds. For example, if you find a couple engaged in a conversation, observe them and ask yourself how they are feeling and how the conversation is going.

You don't need to become a stalker or get into other people's business; simply observe the body language of some people you don't know and draw conclusions.

Alternatively, if you have a friend who wants to help you, ask them to converse with you and use the social cues listed above when they see fit to help you recognize them and understand how the conversation is going. It can also bring in some fun while chatting with your friend!

CHAPTER 11
ADHD AND ROMANTIC RELATIONSHIPS

*A*DHD impacts many aspects of our lives, one of which is our relationships with our partners.

> *"It has been widely maintained that enduring and healthy romantic relationships are critical to quality of life in adulthood, and can buffer the impact of adversity, including psychological disorder. Unfortunately, much research points toward adults with attention-deficit hyperactivity disorder (ADHD) having short-lived and discordant romantic relationships"* (Wymbs B. T., 2021)

How ADHD impacts a relationship can change dramatically according to the type of relationship, the individuals involved, and how ADHD manifests itself. There are dozens of articles and books on the subject, and in this chapter, I don't want to go into detail about every single aspect. Instead, I want to focus on the more significant problems and analyze them from a woman's point of view.

INATTENTION: GETTING BORED AND THE DOPAMINE TRAP

The first problem I want to focus on is getting bored. This happens to most women who have ADHD and is scientifically explainable. We must start from the assumption that it is not true that people with ADHD are unable to focus. Our problem is that we cannot maintain concentration for extended periods in non-rewarding situations. We tend to stare off into space and think about other things.

The lack of concentration is due to various factors, one of which is dopamine. This neurotransmitter is part of the reward system in our brain. When we do something, our brain releases this substance and we feel satisfied. This leads us to keep doing that thing.

> "ADHD is viewed as a disorder primarily of hyperactive-impulsive behavior and inattention; new theories focus on lack of self-regulation, poor inhibition, and deficient executive functioning as being fundamental to the disorder. Interestingly, poor executive functioning is tied to dopaminergic [meaning related to dopamine] genetics." (Gold M. S., 2014)

The problem with our ADHD brain is that dopamine receptors are lower than in a neurotypical person. So having fewer receptors means we need to release much more dopamine than neurotypical people need to feel the same effects.

This is one of the reasons why our brain is incredibly good at focusing on activities that have a high dopamine reward, such as

- things that are of personal interest.
- things that are challenging.
- things that are new or have an element of novelty.

If you think about the beginning of a relationship, it's very easy to understand that these three things are all present. There is a personal interest in getting to know someone new. We are moving into an uncharted area and developing a new relationship, so there are certainly some challenges.

The beginning of a relationship is a constant release of dopamine, and we work well when our brain is flooded with it.

In short, for neurotypical people, the beginning of a relationship is an exceptional period; for us, it is even more so.

However, as the relationship progresses, these elements slowly disappear. When a relationship matures, the sense of novelty slowly fades, the challenges are less difficult, and we begin to get used to everything that used to give us butterflies in the stomach.

This causes our dopamine level to drop, and we begin to seek rewards in other activities. Therefore, we know that there is a scientific reason that explains one of the factors that leads us to get bored quickly.

As the relationship becomes less dopamine rewarding and our focus shifts to other activities, this can negatively impact our relationship with our partner in various ways.

The non-ADHD partner has become accustomed to a certain level of attention and could experience this relationship phase as us pulling away emotionally and physically. This could make them feel neglected and unloved, leading to unpleasant arguments.

On the other hand, some of us may experience relationships as dopamine boosters, and this is a dangerous area that could lead to looking for our dopamine reward elsewhere.

Sometimes, we pretend everything is fine while trying to recreate what we felt at the beginning of the relationship. Other times, we try to change the other person to make everything perfect again, or we cheat on the partner because it's less painful than ending the relationship.

Many people living with ADHD I have worked with over the years have been caught in this cycle of relationships. It is not easy to get out of it; in some cases, it is not even easy to recognize that we are trapped inside one of these cycles.

There is no simple method; notes left around the house don't help in these cases, and neither do the exercises you could do in a book. The best solution is honesty.

Be honest with your partner about who you are and what you need. Be honest about who your partner is and if they are the right person for you. Explain what you look for in a relationship and your deal-breakers.

Try to contextualize your feelings with the state of your relationship. For example, if you have been with the same person for two years, it will hardly be as wild as it was at the beginning. But there will be things you didn't have in the beginning that only become part of a relationship after you get to know each other deeply.

There is no point in pretending that a relationship is right for you. Instead, try to understand whether you are with a person to feel good and get your dopamine reward or it is the person you want to be with. Be honest with yourself.

But, let's face it: Being honest doesn't solve all problems and is often more challenging than pretending everything is fine. Honesty can lead to more fights, being more selective with people, and feeling lonely. But deluding ourselves that a person is right for us and staying in this vicious cycle will do more damage in the long run.

WE NEED REASSURANCE

Needing reassurance occurs in all relationships, but for most people with ADHD, this need is amplified. The need to be reassured, especially by our partner, is because ADHD is often linked to self-esteem and self-image problems:

> *"A lower self-esteem profile is more common in subjects suffering from ADHD than in healthy controls"* (Mazzone L., 2013).

It is a typical pattern for most women with ADHD to conclude that someone doesn't like them or is angry with them. This happens for various reasons. First, our life is not easy; many of us grow up being rejected or having difficulty socializing. Even for ADHD women who are more sociable, any chance to meet people has a fraction of underlying stress from all the extra work our brains must do to keep up with neurotypical people.

Second, we often feel a sense of guilt or shame. For example, sometimes I realize that I might be annoying to my husband, and I know that many of the behaviors that make me annoying are hard to control. For this reason, I feel guilty because I know he has to put up with me. However, having helped many women with ADHD during my career, I know I'm not the only one. Being in an "ADHD relationship" is not easy for either party, but it can also be enriching.

We often focus on the negatives and overlook how an "ADHD brain" and a neurotypical brain can enrich each other.

Let's do an exercise: Ask your partner for five words to define your relationship. For example, when I asked my husband, these are the five words he chose:

- exciting
- chaotic
- patience
- spontaneous
- fun

Some of these words can have a negative connotation, such as chaotic and patience (meaning he has to be patient with me), but there is no reason to feel bad about this. I know that living with me is sometimes a mess, but my husband stays with me for all the other things that make our relationship worth living.

The fact that I frequently ask for reassurance is one of the downsides of living with someone with ADHD, but it's part of the whole package. He is in for the exciting and spontaneous fun!

If you have a partner, try asking them to describe your relationship in five words. Some of these words might have a negative connotation, but you will see that most will be highly positive. Otherwise, they wouldn't have chosen to be in a relationship with you.

```
┌─────────────────────────────────────────────────────────┐
│  WORDS TO DESCRIBE YOUR RELATIONSHIP:                     │
│                                                           │
│  _____     │
│                                                           │
│  _____     │
│                                                           │
│  _____     │
│                                                           │
│  _____     │
│                                                           │
│  _____     │
│                                                           │
│  _____     │
│                                                           │
└─────────────────────────────────────────────────────────┘
```

FAILURE TO FOLLOW THROUGH

The fact that a woman with ADHD generally loves the new also means that their interests can change rapidly. This in itself is not a problem. On the contrary, seeking new stimuli enriches us as people and pushes us to improve.

However, it can become a problem in a relationship when we start leaving countless projects unfinished or missing our commitments.

Neglecting to meet our commitments can erode the trust in any relationship. If we continually leave unfinished tasks and half-done projects lying around, then it's no wonder that our partners will eventually lose faith in us; they may feel like their home is a mess filled with broken promises.

The practical solution to this problem can be found in the previous chapters. It is, in fact, about having a schedule and knowing how to manage your time. The real issue here is not losing our partner's trust if we fail in our commitments for any reason.

The best thing to do in this case is, as usual, to be honest. If you haven't already, explain to your partner what having ADHD entails. This way, they can help and support you, becoming your accountability buddy. At the same time, they will understand that, despite all your efforts, there will be times when even if you started with all the good intentions in the world, you will never finish painting the living room in teal. (Any reference to actual events is purely coincidental!)

Yes, I convinced my husband that adding some color to the living room was a good idea.

Yes, I dropped the task before completing it, and he had to help me finish it.

IMPULSIVITY

The last problem I want to talk to you about is impulsivity. We've covered this topic before in previous chapters but never from the point of view of what it could do to our relationships.

Impulsivity can manifest itself as a problem in a relationship in two main ways. It can affect our finances or important decisions as a couple.

We talked earlier about impulse buying and how this can be a problem for women with ADHD. Unfortunately, within the couple, this problem can become making purchases, sometimes with prohibitive costs, without discussing it in advance with your partner.

Likewise, making decisions on impulse can lead us to make decisions that we should have first discussed with our partners. Some of these decisions may not be that problematic, like when I visited a travel agency to get an idea of where to go on holiday and returned with tickets to the Canary Islands. You should have seen my husband's face.

But others, like a sudden career change, could create problems within a couple's relationship.

In previous chapters, I've shared techniques to manage your finances better and reduce impulse buys. But, as you may have noticed in this chapter, I am focusing now on communication.

Even if you do your best to manage your impulsiveness, there will be situations where you won't be able to, and you will buy something on impulse or decide on something without pondering too much about the consequences.

We can't help it, but we can be communicative with our partners. We should own our mistakes and be open to reviewing our decisions whenever possible. Having our partner's input on important decisions can help us see the situation from a different point of view. Therefore, we must strive to maintain the right mental flexibility to reconsider our decisions on impulse.

At the same time, explaining our "spontaneity" to our partners can help us avoid misunderstandings. They must understand that our impulse action is not due to an intention to cut them off from important decisions; it is simply due to how our ADHD brain works.

Also, remember that making impulse decisions now and then is fun. For example, we went on the Canary Islands trip and had a fantastic holiday!

But ever since, when it comes to buying vacation tickets, we've been doing it together.

CONCLUSION

Through writing this book, I explored the perseverance and courage of women with ADHD who face immense obstacles yet strive to overcome them. Our brains may be wired differently, but that doesn't stop us from achieving remarkable things.

While living with ADHD can present unique challenges, it is important to recognize that this condition also has positive aspects. Our messiness and chaos are the very things that spark our creativity, drive us to new heights of energy, and embolden us with a fearless spirit of spontaneity. With the right tools and support system, we can learn how to use these traits for success.

With this book, I hope I have been able to give you some more tools to combat the negative aspects of ADHD and, at the same time, appreciate your potential and yourself.

To finish off, I would like to leave you with one last piece of advice. When the world throws expectations at you, don't let them define you. Instead, find a way to be content with yourself and create your path, free of society's standards. Celebrate who you are in life. It's your journey, so make sure every step is one closer to happiness.

ONLINE RESOURCES

If you want to continue using the planning sheets in this workbook, you can download them by scanning the following QR code or using the URL link:

http://bit.ly/3HADFEQ

GLOSSARY

BDNF: Brain-derived neurotrophic factor is a gene that provides instructions to make a protein found in the brain. It plays an essential role in neuronal survival and growth, serves as a neurotransmitter modulator, and participates in neuronal plasticity, which is necessary for learning and memory (S. & N, 2015).

Cool Executive function system (CEFs): Cool (or cold) Executive Function refers to the skills we use when emotions aren't a factor. "Cold EFs involve purely cognitive information processing" (Salehinejad, Ghanavati, Rashid, & Nitsche, 2021).

Executive function system: "Executive functions (EFs) make possible mentally playing with ideas; taking the time to think before acting; meeting novel, unanticipated challenges; resisting temptations; and staying focused. Core EFs are inhibition [response inhibition (self-control—resisting temptations and resisting acting impulsively) and interference control (selective attention and cognitive inhibition)], working memory, and cognitive flexibility (including creatively thinking "outside the box," seeing anything from different perspectives, and quickly and flexibly adapting to changed circumstances)" (A., 2013).

Hot Executive function system (HEFs): Hot Executive Function is used in social and high-emotional situations. "Hot EFs involve the processing of information related to reward, emotion, and motivation" (Salehinejad, Ghanavati, Rashid, & Nitsche, 2021).

Neurogenesis: "Neurogenesis is the formation of neurons de novo, the hallmark of a developing brain. The concept of neurogenesis in adult humans is a controversial topic among researchers in the field of neuroscience. While some researchers report that a sharp drop in neurogenesis occurs as the human brain ages, other researchers report that neurogenesis... persists into old age" (Kumar, Pareek, Faiq, Ghosh, & Kumari, 2019).

Neurotypical: Neurotypical is a neologism used to describe people whose brains develop and function in a standard way, as society expects. The word is widely used in the neurodiversity movement and aims to identify people not affected by autism, ADHD, dyslexia, etc.

Restless legs syndrome (RLS): Restless legs syndrome, also known as Willis-Ekbom disease, is a common condition of the nervous system that causes an overwhelming, irresistible urge to move the legs (restless-legs-syndrome, n.d.).

REFERENCES

A., D. (2013). Executive Functions. Annual Review of Psychology, 135-168.

Aduen P. A., D. T. (2018). Social Problems in ADHD: Is it a Skills Acquisition or Performance Problem? *Journal of psychopathology and behavioral assessment*, 440-451.

Beauchaine T. P., B.-D. I. (2020). ADHD, financial distress, and suicide in adulthood: A population study. *Science advances*.

Cross A., S. D. (2016). Mental contrasting as a behaviour change technique: a systematic review protocol paper of effects, mediators and moderators on health. *Systematic reviews*.

Gold M. S., B. K.-B. (2014). Low dopamine function in attention deficit/hyperactivity disorder. *Postgraduate medicine*, 153-177.

Kennedy DP, G. J. (2009). Personal space regulation by the human amygdala. *Nat Neurosci*.

Kumar, A., Pareek, V., Faiq, M. A., Ghosh, S. K., & Kumari, C. (2019). ADULT NEUROGENESIS IN HUMANS: A Review of Basic Concepts, History, Current Research, and Clinical Implications. *Innovations in clinical neuroscience*, 30-37.

LaCunt, P. A., & Hartung, C. M. (2018). Physical Exercise Interventions for Emerging Adults with Attention-Deficit/Hyperactivity Disorder (ADHD). *ADHD Report*, 1-11.

Littman, E. (2022, November 17). *Gender differences in adhd women vs men*. Additude: https://www.additudemag.com/gender-differences-in-adhd-women-vs-men/

Mazzone L., P. V. (2013). Self-esteem evaluation in children and adolescents suffering from ADHD. *Clinical practice and epidemiology in mental health: CP & EMH*, 96-102.

Plessen K. J., B. R. (2006). Hippocampus and amygdala morphology in attention-deficit/hyperactivity disorder. *Archives of general psychiatry*, 795-807.

Ptacek, R., Weissenberger, S., Braaten, E., Klicperova-Baker, M., Goetz, M., Raboch, J., . . . Stefano, G. B. (2019). Clinical Implications of the Perception of Time in Attention Deficit Hyperactivity Disorder (ADHD): A Review. *Medical science monitor : international medical journal of experimental and clinical*, 3918-3824.

restless-legs-syndrome. (n.d.). www.nhs.co.uk: https://www.nhs.uk/conditions/restless-legs-syndrome/

Roselló B., B. C.-R. (2020). Empirical examination of executive functioning, ADHD associated behaviors, and functional impairments in adults with persistent ADHD, remittent ADHD, and without ADHD. *BMC Psychiatry*.

S., B., & N, D. U. (2015). Brain-derived neurotrophic factor and its clinical implications. *Archives of medical science*, 1164-1178.

Salehinejad, M. A., Ghanavati, E., Rashid, M., & Nitsche, M. A. (2021). Hot and cold executive functions in the brain: A prefrontal-cingular network. *Brain and neuroscience advances*.

Wymbs B. T., C. W. (2021). Adult ADHD and romantic relationships: What we know and what we can do to help. *Journal of marital and family therapy*, 664-681.

Yau, S. Y., Gil-Mohapel, J., Christie, B. R., & So, K. F. (2014). Physical exercise-induced adult neurogenesis: a good strategy to prevent cognitive decline in neurodegenerative diseases? *BioMed research international*.

Made in the USA
Middletown, DE
02 August 2023